Cartoons of the Roaring Twenties

VOLUME TWO

1923-1925

Edited by
R.C. Harvey

FANTAGRAPHICS BOOKS

FOR A HARD DRINKER

FANTAGRAPHICS BOOKS
7563 Lake City Way NE
Seattle, Washington 98115

Edited and produced by R.C. Harvey
Cover design by Dale Yarger
Cover art by John Held, Jr.; colored by Jim Woodring
Published by Gary Groth and Kim Thompson

CARTOONS OF THE ROARING TWENTIES is copyright
© 1992 Fantagraphics Books, Inc. and R.C. Harvey.
Permission to quote or reproduce material herein
for reviews or notices may be obtained by writing the publisher.

First edition: April, 1992

1 3 5 7 9 10 8 6 4 2

ISBN: 1-56097-079-0

Printed in the U.S.A.

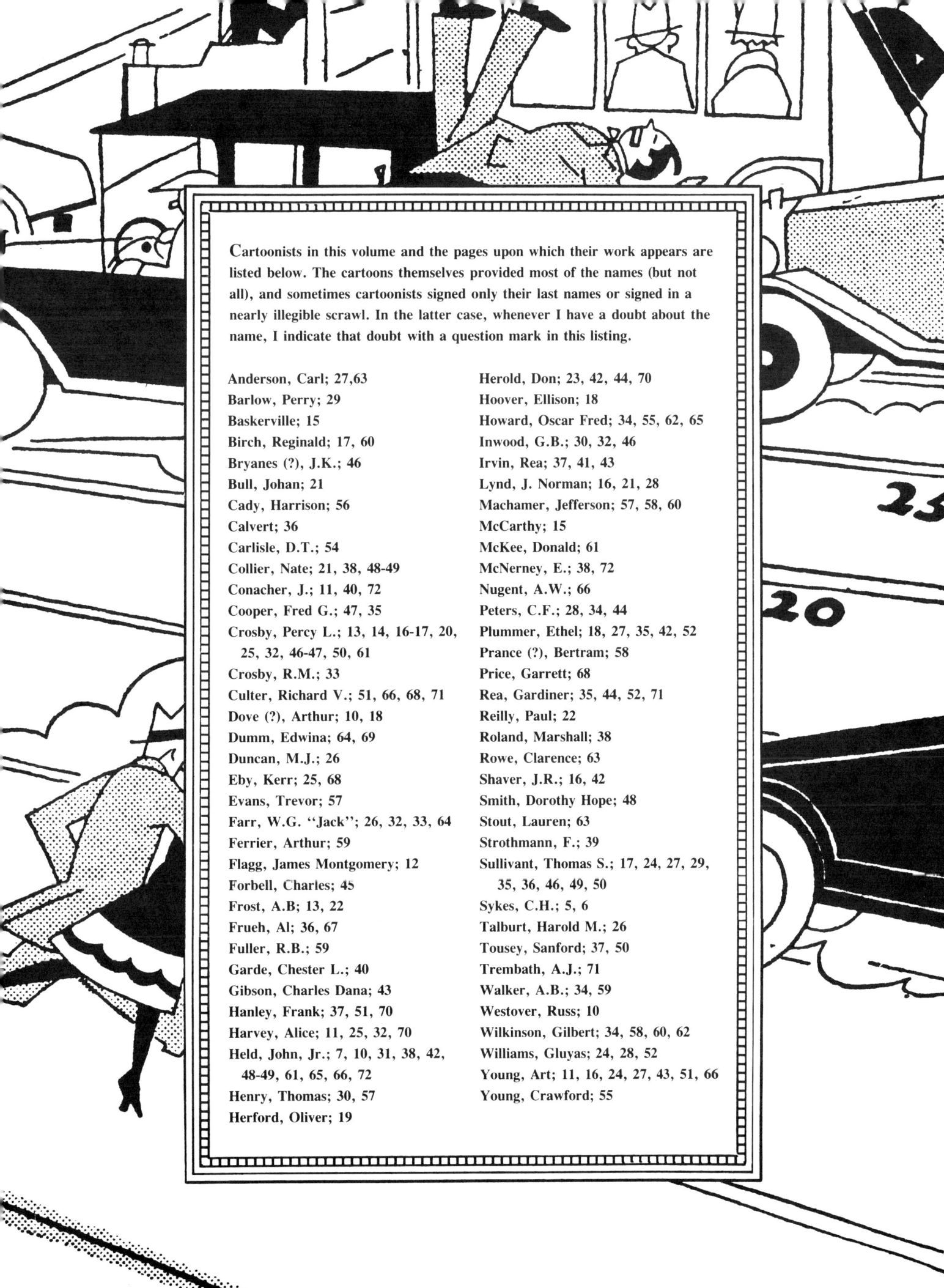

Cartoonists in this volume and the pages upon which their work appears are listed below. The cartoons themselves provided most of the names (but not all), and sometimes cartoonists signed only their last names or signed in a nearly illegible scrawl. In the latter case, whenever I have a doubt about the name, I indicate that doubt with a question mark in this listing.

Anderson, Carl; 27, 63
Barlow, Perry; 29
Baskerville; 15
Birch, Reginald; 17, 60
Bryanes (?), J.K.; 46
Bull, Johan; 21
Cady, Harrison; 56
Calvert; 36
Carlisle, D.T.; 54
Collier, Nate; 21, 38, 48-49
Conacher, J.; 11, 40, 72
Cooper, Fred G.; 47, 35
Crosby, Percy L.; 13, 14, 16-17, 20, 25, 32, 46-47, 50, 61
Crosby, R.M.; 33
Culter, Richard V.; 51, 66, 68, 71
Dove (?), Arthur; 10, 18
Dumm, Edwina; 64, 69
Duncan, M.J.; 26
Eby, Kerr; 25, 68
Evans, Trevor; 57
Farr, W.G. "Jack"; 26, 32, 33, 64
Ferrier, Arthur; 59
Flagg, James Montgomery; 12
Forbell, Charles; 45
Frost, A.B; 13, 22
Frueh, Al; 36, 67
Fuller, R.B.; 59
Garde, Chester L.; 40
Gibson, Charles Dana; 43
Hanley, Frank; 37, 51, 70
Harvey, Alice; 11, 25, 32, 70
Held, John, Jr.; 7, 10, 31, 38, 42, 48-49, 61, 65, 66, 72
Henry, Thomas; 30, 57
Herford, Oliver; 19

Herold, Don; 23, 42, 44, 70
Hoover, Ellison; 18
Howard, Oscar Fred; 34, 55, 62, 65
Inwood, G.B.; 30, 32, 46
Irvin, Rea; 37, 41, 43
Lynd, J. Norman; 16, 21, 28
Machamer, Jefferson; 57, 58, 60
McCarthy; 15
McKee, Donald; 61
McNerney, E.; 38, 72
Nugent, A.W.; 66
Peters, C.F.; 28, 34, 44
Plummer, Ethel; 18, 27, 35, 42, 52
Prance (?), Bertram; 58
Price, Garrett; 68
Rea, Gardiner; 35, 44, 52, 71
Reilly, Paul; 22
Roland, Marshall; 38
Rowe, Clarence; 63
Shaver, J.R.; 16, 42
Smith, Dorothy Hope; 48
Stout, Lauren; 63
Strothmann, F.; 39
Sullivant, Thomas S.; 17, 24, 27, 29, 35, 36, 46, 49, 50
Sykes, C.H.; 5, 6
Talburt, Harold M.; 26
Tousey, Sanford; 37, 50
Trembath, A.J.; 71
Walker, A.B.; 34, 59
Westover, Russ; 10
Wilkinson, Gilbert; 34, 58, 60, 62
Williams, Gluyas; 24, 28, 52
Young, Art; 11, 16, 24, 27, 43, 51, 66
Young, Crawford; 55

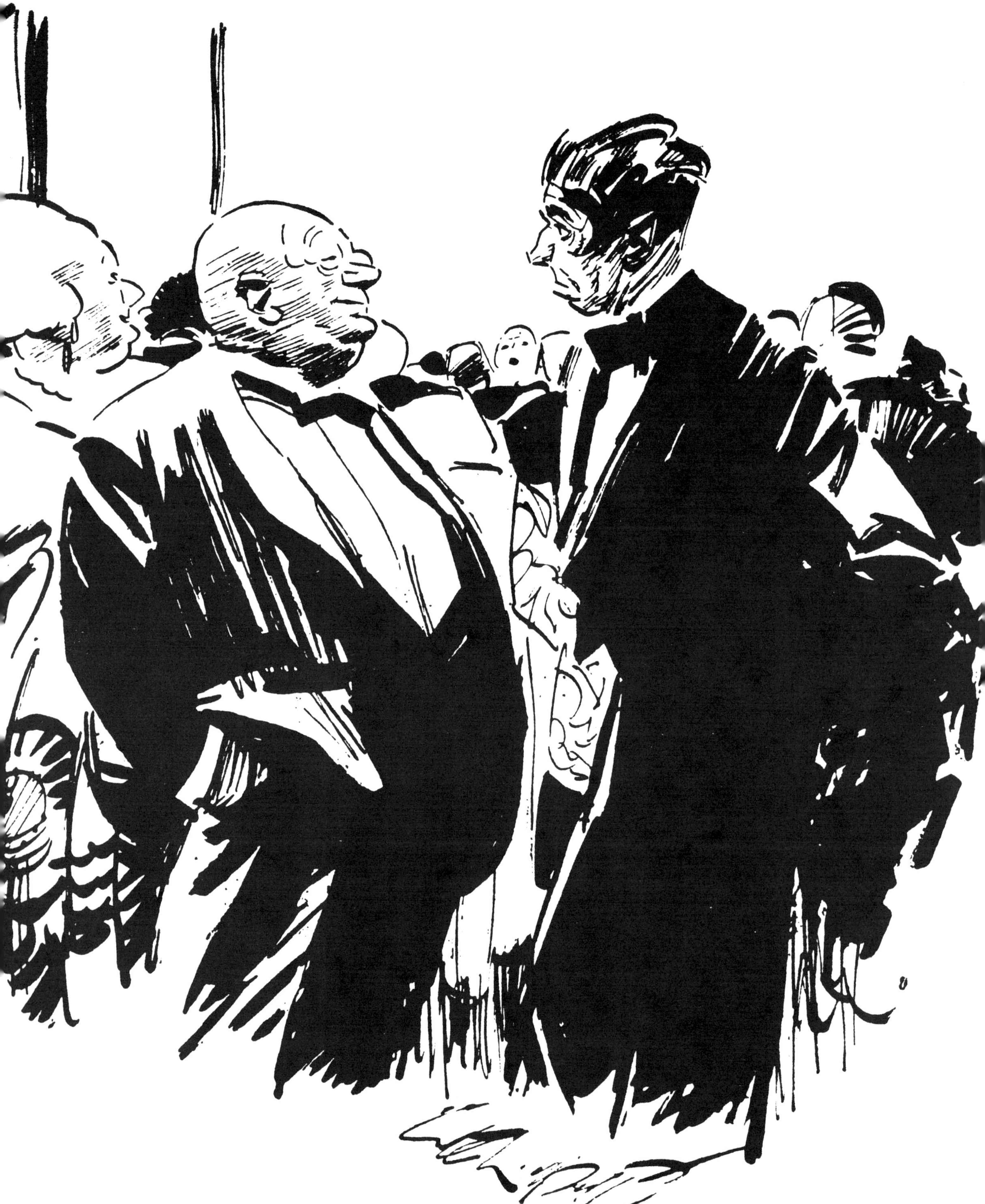

INTRODUCTION

Twentieth Century America didn't begin in 1900 or even in 1901. Until World War I was over, the twentieth century in America was little more than an attic for the nineteenth—full of the dusty and slightly threadbare notions of a fading Victorian Age and the moldy pioneering axioms of the westward movement. But in the 1920s, the salesman replaced the frontiersman in American culture, and with that, Twentieth Century America was born.

Mass production more than anything else created what we know as modern America. Goods produced in the vast quantities made possible by assembly-line methods demanded an entire nation of consumers, and in creating a nation of consumers, the salesman and his lieutenant, the advertising man, created also a national audience. Advertisements concocted in New York to sell products manufactured in Detroit were read in periodicals published in Chicago that were sold from coast to coast. Everywhere, everyone read virtually the same things. Even local newspapers, fed by national wire services, press associations and feature syndicates, were disseminating the same news and ideas in every corner of the land. And the nation's readers were bound even closer together as they became the nation's listeners when the newest marvel of the age swept across the country. The first radio station began by broadcasting the Cox-Harding Presidential election returns November 2, 1920, and was heard only by amateur wireless operators. By the close of the decade, radio had every citizen in its thrall: listeners from Maine to California stopped whatever they were doing every evening to listen for fifteen minutes to "Amos 'n' Andy," one of the earliest radio serials.

During the 1920s, national radio networks and national magazines bound the nation together as nothing else could. Everyone was in the same audience. And as one writer of the day observed, "The national mind became as never before an instrument upon which a few men could play." An audience weary of war and the troubles of the world and with more leisure time than ever before seized eagerly upon whatever distractions mass communications offered. And because the audience was nation-wide, the distractions it seized upon became national crazes. Whenever a new toy or a fad or a scandal engaged the public's fancy, it was promptly and repeatedly on the front pages of every newspaper everywhere, in feature articles in national magazines, and on the airwaves into every home in the land.

By this means, a Frenchman named Emil Coue made his fortune by getting the country to chant his "auto-suggestion" formula for happiness and well-being: "Day after day in every way, I am getting better." Similarly, a Chinese parlor game called Mah Jong took the nation by storm. Next, everyone was singing, "Yes, We Have No Bananas," and then doing crossword puzzles and then marathon dancing or flagpole sitting.

As for scandal, the decade soon had a lulu in the storied film colony on the West Coast. The U.S. was on a movie-going binge. Americans flocked to the country's 17,000 movie houses on the average of once a week to see their favorite screen personalities. Charlie Chaplin was at the peak of his powers. So were Mabel Normand, Douglas Fairbanks, Lillian Gish. Everyone may have been in love with Mary Pickford, the archetypal girl next door, but vast numbers

WHAT NEXT?

of the audience lusted with equal devotion after Theda Bara, the industry's first sex queen. Or Rudolph Valentino, "the great lover." If the movies titillated, the private lives of movie stars absolutely fascinated. In scores of tawdry movie magazines, film folk were depicted as engaged in madcap off-screen depravities—spending fabulous fortunes on wild parties, booze and drugs, ostentatious homes and automobiles. Then, in the fall of 1921, came the sensation that topped all others: the popular comedian Roscoe Conklin "Fatty" Arbuckle was charged with murder when a starlet died after a bedroom interlude with him during one of his celebrated orgies.

Arbuckle was eventually found not guilty, but his career was over. And so was the long bacchanal in Hollywood. Movie moguls, fearing a public reaction that would hurt their box office receipts, decided to clean up the act: they drafted Will Hayes out of Warren Harding's cabinet (which, ironically, would prove as corrupt as Hollywood was debauched) to police the industry's morals, both on screen and off. But sin remained popular in spite of the Hayes Office—both with film stars and with their audience, which conducted itself through much of the decade as if it had just discovered sex.

Some scandals had little to do with the libido. In the summer of 1925, the nation was entertained with daily reports from Dayton, Tennessee, where a school teacher named John Scopes was being tried for teaching evolution. It was the ultimate struggle of the decade—the Modernists against the Fundamentalists. Famed Clarence Darrow offered a nobly intelligent defense, but the jury liked William Jenning Bryan's Bible-thumping prosecution better. Intolerance of all sorts flourished in the twenties. Immigrants, radicals, and all minorities were subject to attack—blacks, Jews, and Catholics in particular. In this environment, the Ku Klux Klan flourish-

ed. Revived, some believe, by the popularity of D.W. Griffith's 1915 *Birth of a Nation*, the KKK grew to a membership of over 4.5 million and dominated political life in the mid-twenties in seven states.

Meanwhile, Prohibition, the Anti-Saloon League's hope for national sainthood, was well on its way to becoming a colossal failure. By 1923, the year the cartoons in this volume began to see print, the supply of illicit liquor was coming into the country in a torrent—across the Canadian border, from ships lying offshore just beyond the 3-mile limit (in "Rum Row"). Instead of being sainted, the nation was besotted.

Breaking liquor laws was commonplace. And almost universally condoned. Edward S. Martin, writing in the nation's venerable humor magazine *Life*, reminded his readers that lawbreakers historically were often heroes: "Among the people who did the most for human liberty and human happiness is a splendid gallery of lawbreakers."

Speakeasies were as much a part of urban life as the growing problem of streets congested by automobile traffic. Speaks were different than saloons: since admittance tended to be restricted to those who knew the password ("Joe sent me"), a clubby membership atmosphere prevailed. Hence, these establishments of the evening's entertainment became "night clubs." (And the admission fee charged to help maintain the hideaway was called, logically, a *couvert* charge.) Each night club tended to develop its own unique ambiance. A one-time movie actress named Texas Guinan made a career as a hostess enlivening a succession of New York's night spots: "Never give a sucker an even break," she advised. And she greeted her customers accordingly: "Hello, sucker," she'd bellow from across the room. For a less boisterous evening, the crowds gathered at Helen Morgan's where the bad booze was made palatable by the torch singer's husky contralto. (Illustrator James Montgomery Flagg explained her appeal best: she was, he said, the composite of all the ruined women in the world.)

All bootleggers were criminals by definition, but they weren't all gangsters. Bootlegging, however, gave gangsters the impetus to organize, and by the end of the dry era, organized crime was an institution. Dapper Johnny Torrio did most of the organizing in Chicago, but when the business threatened to get bloody in 1925, he prudently retired to Italy, leaving his empire to Alphonse Capone. And, sure enough, the business got bloody.

Organized crime didn't find its way into the cartoons of the lawless decade very often: bootlegging could be joked about but not murder. However, in the pages of the old *Life*, Charles H. Sykes sometimes reminded readers about the cloud of criminality hanging over the country. Sykes did political cartoons for the *Philadelphia Evening Ledger* on

"ALAS!" AND "ALACK!"

a daily basis; weekly, he cranked up a cartoon in juicy wash for *Life*, and once a month, he did a page of diminutive pen sketches (like those decorating this Introduction) commenting on the newsiest topics of the past thirty days. One of the star players in these monthly summaries was Sykes' dour and disgruntled Mr. Dry, by whose regular appearance the cartoonist logged the failures of Prohibition.

But if there is any single image that epitomizes the era it is not the funereal Mr. Dry in political cartoons; it is that effervescent bundle of giddy self-assurance, girlish laughter, and unabashed sex appeal—the flapper. The visual symbol of the flapper did not appear widely until she was an accepted type—that is, until about 1923; but she had become a familiar social phenomenon long before then. The typical flapper was a nice girl who was a little fast ("brazen and at least capable of sin if not actually guilty of it," as Shelly Armitage says in her biography of John Held, Jr.). The flapper offended the Older Generation because she defied accepted conventions of decorous feminine behavior. Women's hair had always been long; the flapper wore hers short—"bobbed." She used make-up (which she often applied in public). She wore tight, short dresses which bared her arms and her legs from the knees down; underneath, she wore as little as possible. And on the beach, she resorted to a skin-tight, single-piece costume that didn't cover arms or legs and that therefore left very little of her figure to be imagined. But she did more than symbolize the revolution in feminine fashion and mores: she also embodied the spirit of the times in a way no other figure did. And John Held, Jr., a mere cartoonist, did more to create this revolutionary icon than anyone else. And in the brevity and brilliance of his career, he enacted in his life the meteoric character of the Age of Flaming Youth that he so deftly illustrated with his pen.

Held had come to New York from Salt Lake City in 1910, seeking a serious career as a sculptor, but he took work with advertising firms in order to make a living and sent for his wife Myrtle as soon as he felt secure. Formerly society editor for the *Salt Lake City Tribune*, Myrtle had a kind of self-assurance that her husband, at that time, lacked. Seeing commercial value in the comic sketches Held made after hours, she took them around to magazines and sold them. By 1915, Held's work was appearing in *Judge*, *Life*, *The Smart Set*, and *Vanity Fair*. (For years, his drawings were signed "Myrtle Held" or "Babette" because those who first bought them had believed that the woman who peddled them had also drawn them, and Myrtle, rather than give a tedious explantation, had played along, scrawling her name on her husband's unsigned work.)

After World War I, Held began to develop a new drawing style to portray the new social order that was emerging in the post-war years. The Younger Generation, disillusioned by the brutishness of the conflict and the sordid politics of

HOW THAT BRAT HAS GROWN!

its aftermath (which demonstrated that the world was no more safe for democracy than it had been before the War), threw itself into cynical pursuit of some unattainable anodyne for their spiritless existence. Affecting a bored detachment beyond their experience of life, the Young plunged into endless rounds of drinking and pointless escapading, making merry desperately as if there were no tomorrow. Focusing on their antics, Held captured their insouciance with the simple elegance of his line, their youth with perfectly spheroid heads proportionately too large for their bodies. Initially, Held's belles were roundish, almost plump (as on page 10 herein), but at the apogee of their evolution, they were skinny approximations of their sex, emblematic of a sort of perpetual adolescence (see, for instance, page 72). As skirts became shorter, he exaggerated the effect by making his girls' legs longer and slenderer, giving them the gangling coltish appearance of youth. And so was the apotheosis of the flapper achieved.

Humorist Corey Ford maintained that Held actually invented the flapper by supplying the Young with a prototype: "Each new Held drawing was pored over like a Paris fashion plate, girls cropped their hair and rouged their cheeks and shortened their skirts to be in style, galoshes and raccoon coats were indispensable to every male undergraduate wardrobe. So sedulously did we ape his caricatures that they lost their satiric point and came to be a documentary record of our times."

Without question, Held defined the spirit of the decade. More than any other cartoonist, Held captured in his graphic abstractions the fashions and fads of the collegiate jazz age. His leggy flappers with noses in the air and hose rolled at the knee and his bell-bottomed sheiks with their hair plastered tight to cue-ball heads personified the Younger Generation to a nation of readers. Sophisticated and vaguely dissolute, his short-skirted cuties were insatiable neckers, and their tuxedo-clad escorts inveterate social bootleggers, a flask on every hip. And the drawings were rendered with matching elan—delicate, fragile lines in bold contrast against arresting solid blacks.

Held's drawings appeared regularly in all the most popular magazines. At the height of his fame, editors begged for his work. Theatrical caricaturist Al Hirschfeld, one of Held's closest friends, tells of watching Held open his morning mail—each of 20 or 30 envelopes containing a check for hundreds or thousands of dollars.

By this time, the would-be sculptor was trapped by the commercial and economic demands of his success. With a new wife in charge of their social life, Held had to support a lavish "roaring twenties" lifestyle, complete with weekend parties and mansions in Westport and Palm Beach. The work ethic of his Mormon upbringing very much operative in the cartoonist's mind, he was an absentee merry-maker: while his wife and friends partied through the nights, he hunched over his drawing board to earn the money that financed the fun.

Identifying intimately with the frivolity of the twenties, Held didn't make the transition to the grim depression times that followed. Suddenly, magazine editors no longer wanted his work, and his cartoons soon disappeared from the national scene. In 1931, he had a nervous breakdown.(Hirschfeld says his friend was done in by changing feminine fashion: "The long skirt imported from Paris did it. Held's drawing of a girl in a long dress was ludicrous. Russell Patterson, an illustrator, replaced Held's flapper with a cleverly drawn anatomically persuasive girl in a tight-fitting, transparent,

FROM A FRESHMAN'S LETTER HOME
"DEAR MOTHER: —EVERY MORNING I EXERCISE WITH DUMBBELLS."

long dress." But Hirschfeld, with the caricaturist's occupational flair, is exaggerating, over-simplifying. Patterson, as we'll see in the next volume of this series, was established as a delineator of fashionable life in the twenties well before hemlines fell and the stock market crashed and ended the party.)

During the hard-scrabble thirties, Held wrote fiction and illustrated it, designed stage sets, hosted a radio variety show, and became a serious artist—watercolors and sculpture, at last. He married his fourth wife in 1942, and they retired to a small working farm in New Jersey. Following World War II, Held was rediscovered and enjoyed considerable reputation until his death (of throat cancer) in 1958. But his work, documenting an era, lives on.

Held's style was unique—without precedent or imitation. But as this volume attests, he was not the only distinctive cartooning stylist who emerged in the Roaring Twenties. The cartoons herein were assembled mostly from the 1923-25 pages of the old *Life*, supplemented slightly by a few from 1924-25 issues of its rival, *Judge*. Many of the same cartoonists appeared in both publications (and in *The New Yorker* when it began), and while not all cartoonists of the day were represented in these magazines, the cartoons in this anthology are nonetheless representative of the period—illustrative of the spirit of the times and of the state of the art of cartooning.

One of the most individualistic pen techniques in the history of cartooning belonged to Percy L. Crosby, whose famed newspaper strip character, Skippy, debuted in the pages of *Life* in 1923. The March 15 issue announced Skippy Skinner's imminent advent with the picture and copy shown here (next page); the following week, the kid arrived in all his spunky impudence as depicted on page 14. Crosby's sketchy, unlabored line has a ferocious energy, the vitality born of pen tearing breakneck across paper, and Crosby's subjects were imbued with that energy even when drawn in repose. And the cartoonist's distinctive style of drawing is as much a part of his nine-year-old protagonist's character as the gags that gave him personality. Strangely, Skippy's anachronistic costume belies his character: attired always in an English schoolboy's gown (smock-like jacket), high Eton collar with flaring bow-ribbon tie, and short pants, Skippy should be a well-behaved momma's boy. Only his shapeless hat, tilted rakishly—provocatively, almost belligerently—over his eyes and his down-at-the-ankle socks betray him as a boy's boy, rowdy and roguish and just a trifle quarrelsome, who swaggers into view with his hands jammed deep into his pockets, strutting his neophyte machismo. Skippy proved so popular that Crosby, who owned the copyright on the character, syndicated a daily strip version, starting June 23, 1925. Distributed at first by bush league syndicates, "Skippy" was eventually taken up by Hearst—a Sunday page in 1926; then in 1929, the dailies.

Largely self-taught while on the job as staff cartoonist and reporter-artist for the *New York Globe* (briefly) and then (for several years) for Pulitzer's *World*, Crosby had too much energy to confine his efforts solely to his strip. He was a creative volcano, waiting to blow. During his peak years of production (between, say, 1925 and 1940), he spewed out 14 books—novels (often about Skippy, with whom the Brooklyn-bred Crosby identified very closely), poetry, and essays on philosophy, politics, literature, and art. He also painted in oil and watercolor, and he crusaded for individual rights and freedom of the press—and against Prohibition, bootleggers, gangsterism, atheism, naval disarmament, and pacificism. When editors wouldn't print his diatribes on such subjects, he took full-page ads in large metropolitan newspapers to air his views. (Skippy, his alter ego, often philosophized on Crosby's favorite subjects. Once when an editor had the temerity to object to Crosby's fulminating in the strip, Crosby wrote back: after wondering if the editor permitted his readers to stay up past 9 p.m., he told the editor he took orders from no one, and then he nonchalantly removed the paper from the strip's list of subscribers.)

Tragically, Crosby was eventually consumed by his passions. His crusades became more furious, and he began to imagine that the objects of his tirades were plotting to ruin him. Increasingly throughout the forties, he made Skippy his mouthpiece, and finally, King Features sought to rein him in. Crosby wouldn't agree to the terms of the renewal contract he was offered, so the strip died on December 8, 1945. Four years later—his marriage in shambles, separated from his children, income dwindling to nothing, unable to find a public forum, and drinking heavily—Crosby attempted suicide. Diagnosed as a paranoid schizophrenic, he was committed to a mental institution where he spent the last 16 years of his life in bitter isolation from all responsive human contact, desperately trying to secure his release (he was scarcely insane by the standards of the next generation), writing tracts in lucid, often brilliant prose that no one would ever read, and drawing pictures of favorite subjects—dancers, skaters, horses. But never Skippy. He never drew Skippy again.

Elsewhere on these pages is another figure familiar to newspaper comic strip readers—Grandma from Edwina's "Cap Stubbs and Tippie." Edwina is Edwina Dumm, who had begun her cartooning career in about 1915 as editorial cartoonist for the *Monitor* in Columbus, Ohio. (She was the nation's first female political cartoonist—an authentic *rara*

Have you a little Demon in your home?

MEET SKIPPY SKINNER, the latest offspring of P. L. Crosby, who will give him his start in LIFE on March 22nd, with weekly appearances thereafter. What a kid! And what a kidder! You'll love the little rascal as your own—more so, if anything, for you won't have to pay for the furniture he breaks. "Mischief" is his favorite alias, and tricks are things he is always up to nothing else but.

avis at a time when women could not yet vote.) She came to New York in 1917 on the tenuous strength of her intuition about syndicate head George Matthew Adams: he once told her that he liked her drawings of dogs, so she thought he would buy her work. She was right, and "Cap Stubbs," a strip about a boy and his dog, was soon launched. Edwina did other occasional illustration, including a regular page about one of her dogs for *Life*. The first of these, from the issue of July 16, 1925, appears here on page 64.

Although the dog was called Socrates in his first appearance, his name wasn't mentioned again, and by the summer of 1929, readers had long forgotten (apparently) that he even had a name. *Life* ran a contest that summer to name the animal and in the August 31 issue announced the winning submission—Sinbad. (Sinbad led a double life: he was so lively and cute that Adams asked Edwina to replace Tippie, the short-haired mutt in her strip, with a version of the fluffier-looking Sinbad. Edwina was flabbergasted: how could she separate her boy hero from his beloved dog? It was unthinkable, but she eventually solved the ticklish assignment ingeniously: the original Tippie got lost and then was found by a little cripple boy, who became so fond of the dog that when Cap at last came to reclaim his pet, not even he could bear to part them. Instead, he found a new dog, which he also called Tippie.)

Another of *Life*'s cartoonists who did a newspaper feature was Gluyas Williams. Rendered in Williams' stolid black and chaste white manner, "Fred Perley," a panel cartoon, debuted in 1923 and continued for 25 years. Williams, who had graduated in 1911 from Harvard where he'd been art editor of the notorious *Lampoon*, had drawn for the *Boston Journal* and edited art for *Youth's Companion* before starting to submit regularly his patented comic tableaux to *Life* in 1919.

Arthur B. Frost, on the other hand, was near the end of his career. A contributor to *Life* for three decades or more,

Frost made his most enduring mark in American visual arts by doing the definitive illustrations for Joel Chandler Harris' Uncle Remus stories in the 1890s. Highly regarded for his paintings of sporting scenes, Frost also excelled at pen drawings of animals and eccentric rustics. Winsor McCay, famed creator of the fanciful "Little Nemo in Slumberland," considered Frost "the greatest comic draftsman in the history of the country." He was noted among his contemporaries for his comic depictions of black people, one of which I've included here for the sake of the record (page 13). Cartoons of this sort were common in the 1920s although by no means prevalent.

The benighted society that found humor in such cruel caricatures is, I hope, becoming a thing of the past, and I have no wish to extend its vitality any by bringing forward these savage old stereotypes. Still, to leave cartoons like this out of this collection altogether is to suppress them as well as an unsavory part of our past—and thereby to misrepresent history. And just as we need memory of the Jewish Holocaust to remind us how monstrous we can be if our ethnocentricities are permitted unrestrained sway, we need a caricature by Frost to remind us that racial stereotypes like his were wholly fictitous: they had their origins in minstrel show characters that were invented without much reference to real people by white men in blackface to promote their comic purposes on stage.

Psychologically, the blackface comedy of the nineteenth century stage served to quell anxieties in white audiences that wished to justify slavery or (after resolution of that issue) that feared an emerging black populace. In the 1920s, the cartoons of Frost and others may have served much the same psychological funciton. Ironically, at the same time that Frost's cartoons were making people laugh at lazy ignorant rural blacks, the staff of *Life* and much of the rest of the population of the nation's most urbane center often found its entertainment in the city's nightlub mecca, Harlem. At the time, Harlem was a black metropolis, the black capitol of the world, and the scene of a literary and cultural flowering that become known as the Harlem Renaissance. Elsewhere in the country, blacks were suffering persecution unparalleled since Reconstruction. Between 1918 and 1927, over 400 blacks were killed by the lynch mobs that were common in some rural areas. And so to assuage their fear and shame at these developments, white Americans laughed at cartoons like Frost's.

It's no good contending, as some historians have, that cartoonists who drew cartoons with racial and ethnic stereotypes were having innocent fun with minorities they otherwise respected. They respected those minorities no more than any other white Anglo Saxon protestant of their time. And no less. The were simply no different in this regard than the population at large. But they ridiculed the Ku Klux Klan mercilessly—and consistently.

Other unique stylists whose work is represented here include Gilbert Wilkinson, whose brilliant studies in black and white and supple line appeared most frequently in *Judge*; Fred G. Cooper, whose antic calligraphy enlivened the pages of *Life* (and inspired the typeface named for him); Gardner Rea, drawing in a manner only vaguely evocative of the stark simplicity of his later style; Art Young, whose gentle and genial nature is better reflected in his cartoons for *Life* than in his savage attacks on social injustice in *The Masses*; T.S. Sullivant, whose anthropomorphic animals and Biblical buffoons had been committing hilarities in *Life* since 1891; and Dorothy Hope Smith, who gained immortality with her drawing of a baby's face for Gerber's baby food label. Also in these pages, we can see the forever frazzled-looking Jefferson Machamer girl, whose figure not even the straight lines of flapper fashion could shroud; the Alice Harvey girl, a modest maiden only slightly dingy; and the Ethel Plummer girl, a dangerously saucy flapper. And we can find some of the first of a series of nostalgic cartoons by which Richard V. Culter created "The Gay Nineties."

In addition to showcasing the work of some of the best of the decade's cartoonists, the three volumes in this series of *Cartoons of the Roaring Twenties* also reveal the state of the art of the single-panel (or "gag") cartoon during a critical period of its evolution. Until the 1920s the gag cartoon was merely an illustration for comic dialogue that appeared underneath it in a series of verbal exchanges. By the end of the decade, the single-speaker caption had supplanted the multiple-speaker caption, and a new kind of cartoon emerged. In the old gag cartoon, the humor resided chiefly in the words of the caption; in fact, the picture was often entirely superfluous to the joke. In the modern gag cartoon, words and picture are interdependent: the significance of the drawing is made clear only by the utterance of one of the characters in the drawing; by the same token, the import of the utterance is evident only when the picture above it is understood. Words and picture thus blend to create comedy that neither alone provokes.

Many of the cartoons in this volume demonstrate the evolution in thinking by which pictures became integral to the humor of the gag cartoon. In the 1920s, a kind of "visual wit" distinguished many cartoons. In such cartoons as Don Herold's on pp. 23 or 70 or Jack Farr's on p. 26, the humor arises entirely from the cleverness of the pictures. And in cartoons like Ellison Hoover's on p. 18, the words draw attention to the picture, which, in turn, delivers the joke. Ditto Held's "Outlines of History" cartoon on p. 31 (inspired by H.G. Wells' best-selling book with that title).

Cartoonists doubtless noticed the greater comic impact in cartoons of such verbal-visual blending and began to strive for that effect. Despite the long-standing tradition that Harold Ross and his cartoonists at *The New Yorker* invented the single-speaker captioned cartoon, the evolution of the gag cartoon along these lines was evident long before Ross's magazine appeared on the scene on February 21, 1925. The eccentric Ross's insistence on such niggling details as being able to tell which of the figures in a drawing was speaking no doubt helped to focus his cartoonists' efforts in the direction of single-speaker captions, and the success, by the end of the decade, of his magazine over the foundering *Life* and *Judge* surely established the form even if it did not invent it. But even *The New Yorker* published multiple-speaker captioned cartoons through much of the decade. Still, it was clear that the old illustrated verbal witticism was on its way out, and the cartoons herein helped to show the way.

In keeping with the evolutionary spirit that informs the gag cartoon during the 1920s, the cartoons in this volume march through its pages in roughly the order in which they first appeared, the end of each year punctuated by a Christmas cartoon. The parade begins immediately to the right.

— R.C. HARVEY
August 28, 1990
Champaign, Illinois

"What are your college colors?"
"Orange and gin."

"Where can I be vaccinated so that it will not show?"
"On the ear."

Travel broadens one—

But what's the use?

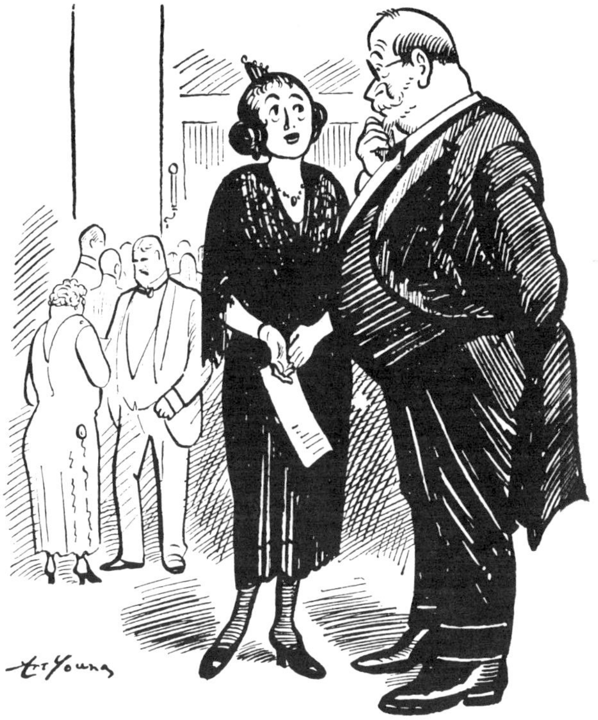

Making Conversation

LADY: *But don't you think, Professor, that sin is better than it was?*

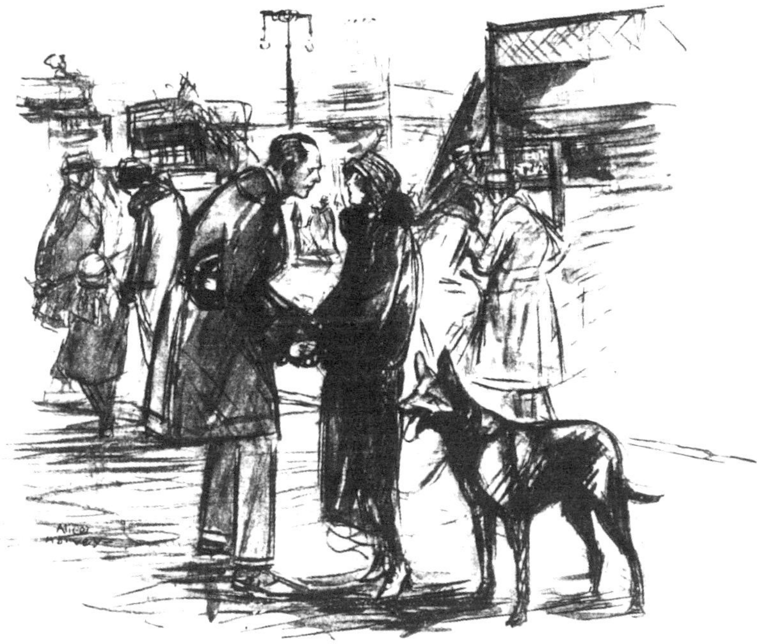

HE (passionately): *You are trying to forget me!*
"No—I'm trying to remember you."

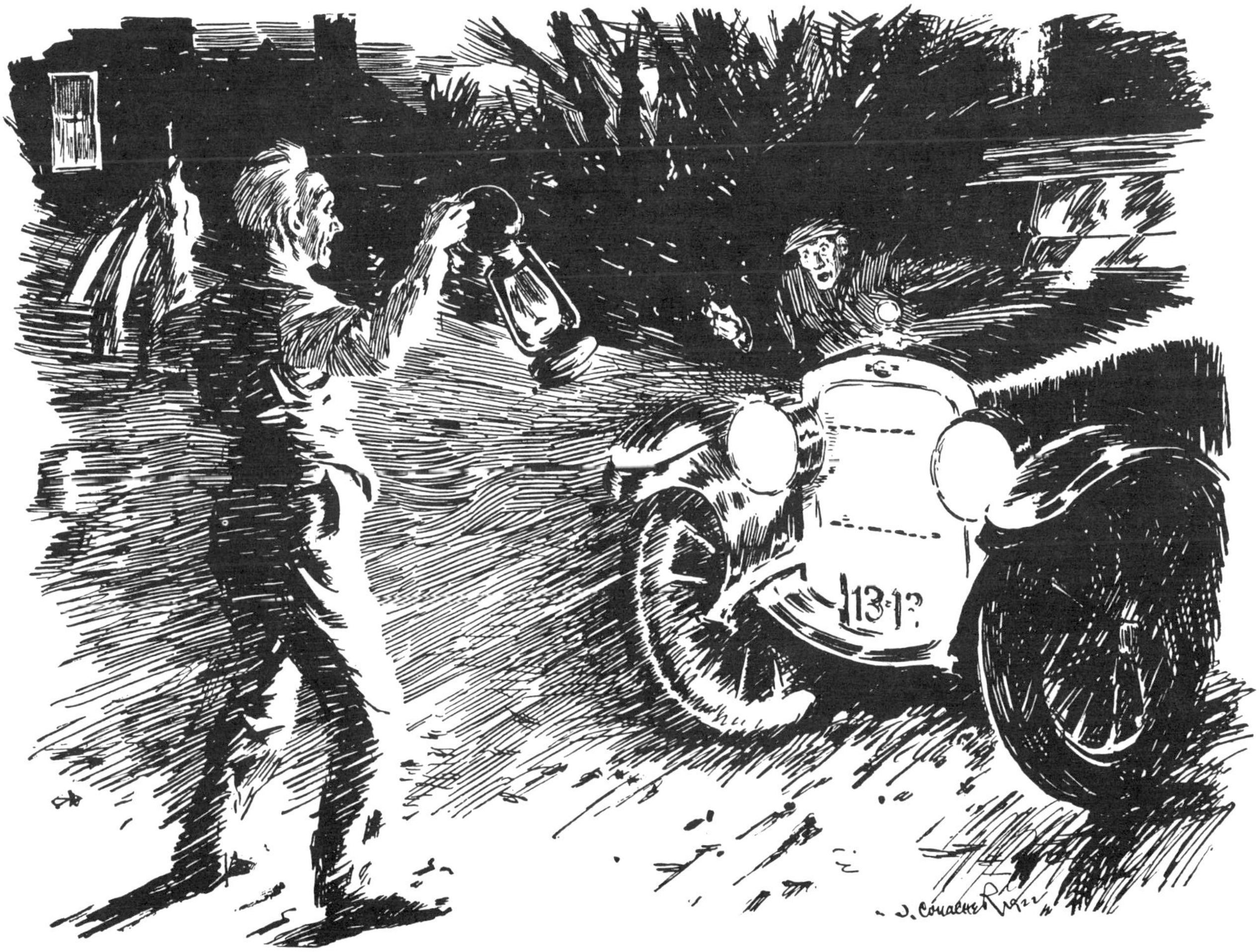

13-1?

MOTORIST (frantically flagged on a lonely road): *What's the matter? Is the bridge out?*
NATIVE: *It's my missus, mister. She's goin' to prayer meeting' an' she's got some grease on her coat. She wants to know would you let her have a haff-a-pint o' gasoline.*

You and Your Cigarettes

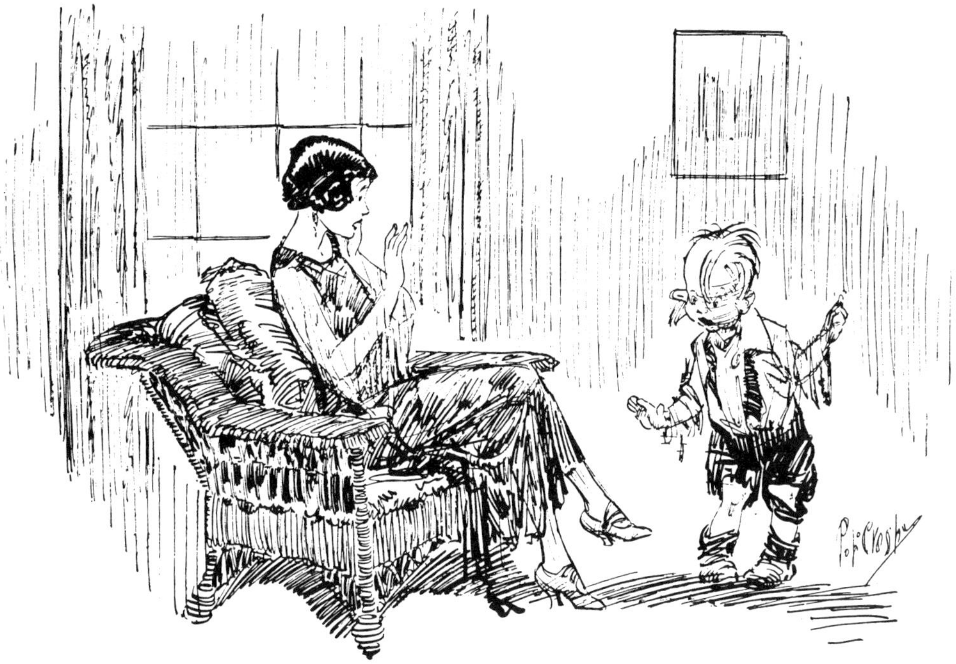

"Didn't I tell you that I would punish you if I found you fighting? What were you arguing about?"
"Willie said you were ten years older'n his mother."
"Ten years! The idea!"
"Don't cha worry, Ma! I learned him to say ya were twenty years older."

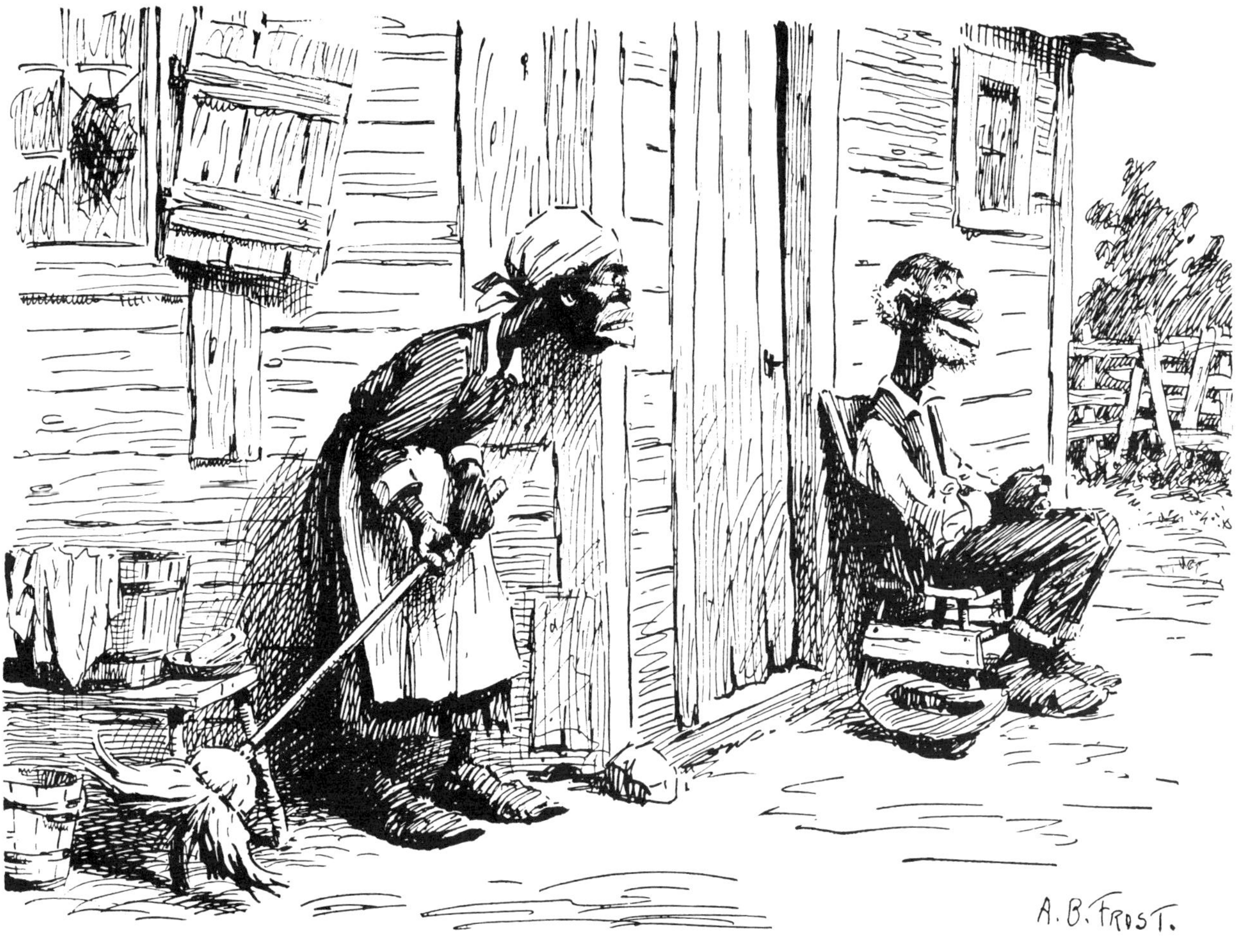
A. B. FROST.

The Coming Storm

MOSE (for the seventeenth time): *Every day, in every way, I'se gitten bettah an' bettah.*

"Lissen, Sockey! The grocer's just put some choc'late bars on the counter, go in and ask for something he don't keep an' I'll wait for ya. Ain't that a good idea?"

"I got a better idea—You go in!"

Skippy: A package of bird-seed, Mr. Blatz.
Mr. Blatz: Bird-seed? You were in for that a couple of times, I think.
Skippy: Yes, sir!

Mr. Blatz: Bird-seed? Bird-seed? Wait, I'll look in the back.

? ? ? ? ?

! ! ! ! !

"Papa! Skippy's swipin' our chawklet, swipin' our chawklet!"

! ! ! !—!—!

Mother's Voice: Is that you, Skippy?
Skippy: Y—yes, M—mama!

Mother's Voice: Well, I want you to go to the grocer's and get me a package of birdseed. Papa just brought home a canary.

Skippy—No. 1

ENTHUSIAST: *She's a past mistress of* legato.
DOWAGER: *Dear me, those fickle Italians.*

"My dear, I'm perfectly devastated. I can't get any endive anywhere for my dinner to-night, and it's the only salad that will match my new frock."

"Don't you wish you could do that, Willie? I betcha it's awfully hard to do."
"Hard nothin'! He only knocks off what he don't need."

Cupid's Busy Day

"I told ye not to chew gum while ye was blowin' it."

"Don't you think he's done you justice?"
"Me? Say, I don't want justice; I want mercy."

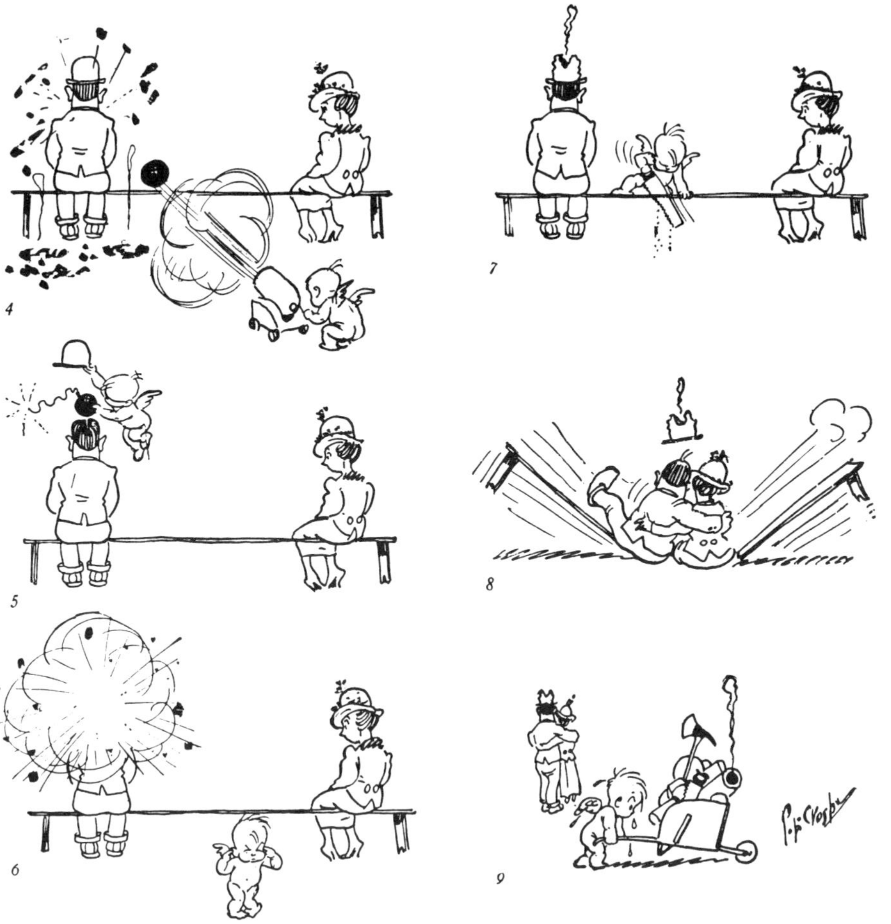
4
7
5
8
6
9

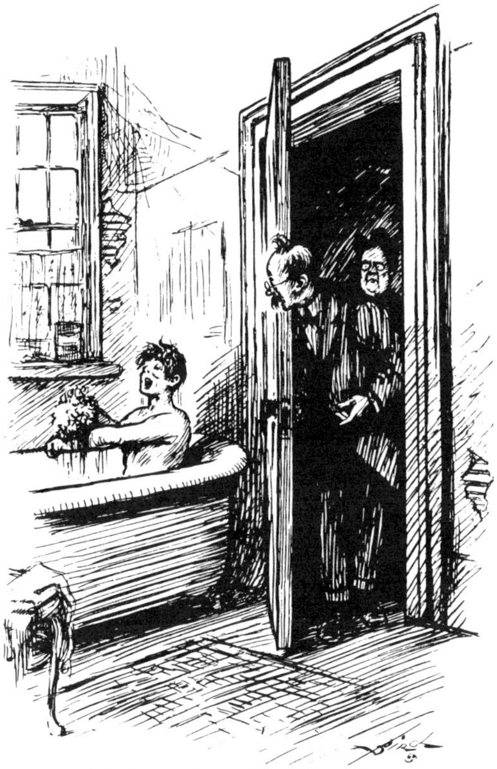

Nocturne in a Boarding House

"Beanpole, why do you sing in the bath?"
"The door won't lock."

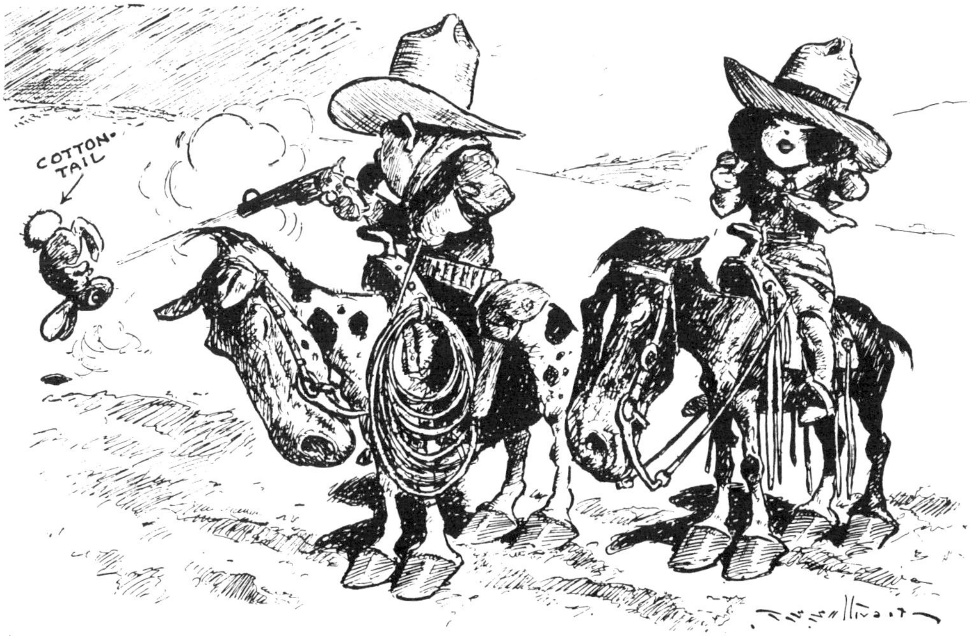
COTTON-TAIL

"Ye say ye lost yer powder-puff, miss? Jest a minute and I'll fix ye up with a new one."

HE BURNED HIS BRITCHES BEHIND HIM.

Motivation

MISS FORME: *Will this bathing suit shrink?*
CLERK: *Positively not.*
MISS FORME: *Show me a cheaper brand.*

SHE: *At this distance it's hard to tell the men from the women.*
HE: *Yes, at this distance it's not worth while trying.*

Impossible Adventures
No. 3—The Lady from Missouri

SKIPPY: *What's the matter? You ain't playin' the bag like you used to did—give us your glove!*

SKIPPY: *Now watch me! All right, fellers! Let's have a few.*

SKIPPY: *Now do you understand how to do it?*

Skippy—No. 13

His Limit

WIFE: *How many cigars a day are you smoking now:*
HUSBAND: *Oh, just enough to show the doctor his advice was wrong.*

"Maybe if we'd smoked cigarettes instead of these insidious pipes we'd a' been bank presidents or railroad directors or sumpin' worth while, too."

THE PEEVED PEDESTRIAN AND THE
OBLIGING MOTORIST

"Jack, do you believe that figures don't lie?"
"Well, those two there appear perfectly truthful as far as I can see."

THAT LEARNING-TO-RIDE FEELING

FIRST LADY: *Shoo!*
SECOND LADY: *Sing the Toreador's Song; maybe that will scare him.*

THE OL' SWIMMIN' HOLE

FOR A HARD DRINKER

FOR A CHRONIC KICKER

FOR A CHORUS GIRL

FOR A MULE OWNER

FOR A HANDY MAN AROUND THE HOUSE

FOR A TRAFFIC COP

FOR A RECKLESS DRIVER

FOR A GOAT FANCIER

FOR A FOOTBALL MAN

FOR A BOOKWORM

FOR AN ACROBAT

FOR AN IDLER

Designs for Appropriate Book-Ends

The Price of Vanity
"Why is Minnie jumping about so?"
"She had her tail bobbed in the spring and now she can't keep the flies off her."

UTTER DISRUPTION OF THE GERMAN CUSTOMS OFFICE ON THE
RETURN OF A TRAVELER FROM AMERICA

CUSTOMER: *How much are them bathin' beauty postcards, Lem?*
VILLAGE GROCER: *Dunno as I want to sell 'em, Ed—I kinda like to look at 'em of an evenin'.*

JUNKMAN: *Hello, Silas. Got some junk there to sell?*
FARMER: *Go wan—there ain't no more junk, it's all anteeks now.*

"*Well, I guess I know how to make one now.*"

"*Oh, look! Somebody's left the telephone running!*"

REMEMBER THE LENGTH OF THE CHURCH AISLE?

"Huh! Any dumbbell kin see that!"

Paid in Full

"This bootlegging must be a good business. You're probably making a fortune."
"Aw, it ain't de coin what counts so much wit' me, lady. It's de people you meet."

"What's he been doing?"
"Overtrowin' the Govermunt."

"Kathleen plays bridge like an amateur."
"Goodness! Is she as lucky as that?"

NONE SO BLIND AS THOSE THAT WILL NOT SEE

THE PUP: *Well, I wounded him, anyhow!*

God Rest Ye, Merrie Gentlemen

THE CUSTOM OF SINGING CAROLS ALWAYS LOOKS SO ATTRACTIVE ON THE PRETTY CHRISTMAS CARD BUT—

SOMEHOW, WHEN WE TRY IT OUT IN OUR SUBURB THE ROMANCE SEEMS TO GO OUT OF IT.

"How d'you come to be sleepin' in the parks?"
"Oh, I used to manufacture corsets."

"Is there anything else I can eliminate from this costume?"
"Well, my dear, you won't really need the mask."

ANOTHER SUSPICIOUS CHARACTER

DR. MONK: *Take a hundred and fifty of these pills with five gallons of hot lemonade before you go to bed to-night and let me know how you feel in the morning.*

BIG SISTER: *Is it 'alf price for me, please?*
CASHIER: *Yes.*
"*Will yer please give me one 'alf ticket, one quarter, and one for nothin'?*"

"*If you ain't in a hurry, ma'am, I'll drive around him.*"

OUTLINES OF HISTORY

Take, for instance, The Outlines of the Egyptian, The Phairest for the Pharaoh's—what?

—then the Classical Outlines of the Greek as told in Song, Story, and Priceless Marbles

—now the Outlines during the Reign of Louis

—which all leads up to Modern times or, what we might term, the Synthetic Gin Period, thus proving that History is not at all interesting without lines.

Drawn by JOHN HELD, JR.

"That's no way to do! The man shoulda never started to build him a house if he didn't know how to finish it."

JUDGE: *Thirty days!*
INCORRIGIBLE: *Hath September, y' Honor.*

THE MORNING PAPER

WHEN THE FORESTS ARE GONE

"*Do you like Kipling?*"
"*Why—I don't know. How do you kipple?*"

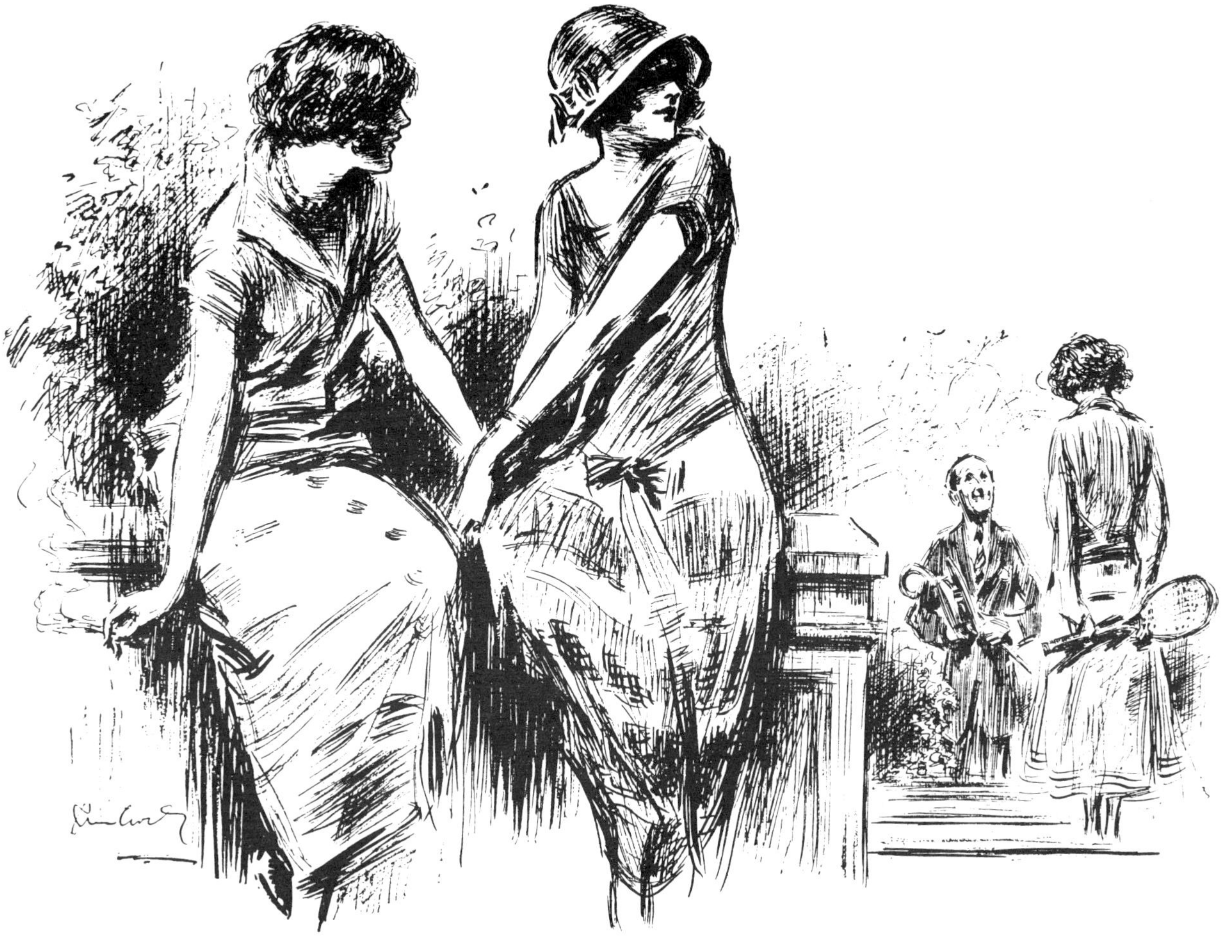

New Models for Old

"How long has Marian had that *man?"*
"That's the one she got last year."
"Well, It's about time she traded him in."

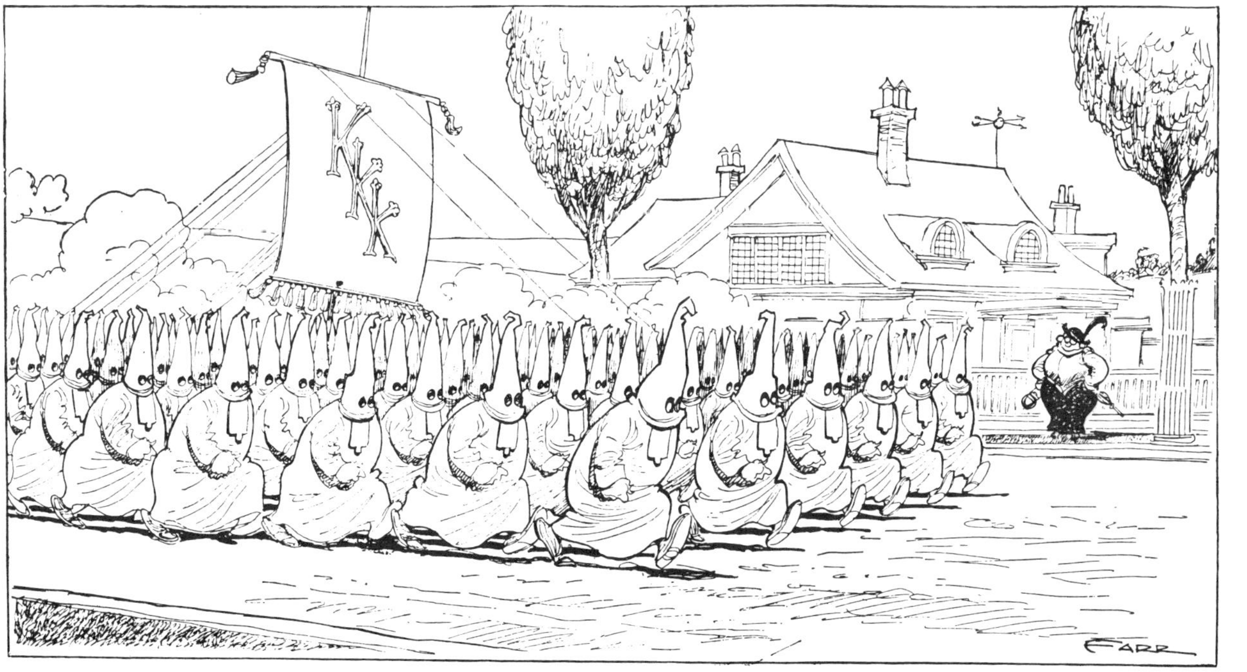

THE KLANSMAN'S WIFE: *A lot of fun it is for me watching John parade! I don't know when to clap.*

SHERLOCK HOLMES, JR.: *She's going fishing.*
YOUNG WATSON: *Fishing? Then why the bathing suit?*
SHERLOCK HOLMES, JR.: *That's her bait.*

GEORGE: *Don't you love water sports?*
GEORGETTE: *Yes, but I am rather particular about the ones I go in for.*

BETTY: *Are you going to smoke when you grow up?*
KITTY: *Yes, if my hands are pretty.*

DINER: *I say, Miss, I'm in a hurry.*
WAITRESS: *Don't let me detain you.*

"Well, Hepsy, I've sold th' house. They're a-goin' t' begin tearin' of it down next week."
"My, my, Hir'm, I'll never in th' wide world git it cleaned in time!"
"Tch! Tch!"

NATIVE: *Be ye tourists?*
WEARY MOTORIST: *No; detourists.*

MRS. DUCK: *I can't find that egg I produced this morning anywhere.*
MRS. HEN: *You must have mislaid it.*

EQUAL RIGHTS FOR MEN

WHY DOES A CHICKEN CROSS THE ROAD?

DESCENDANT OF MRS. O'LEARY'S COW: *Ah, what's the use?*

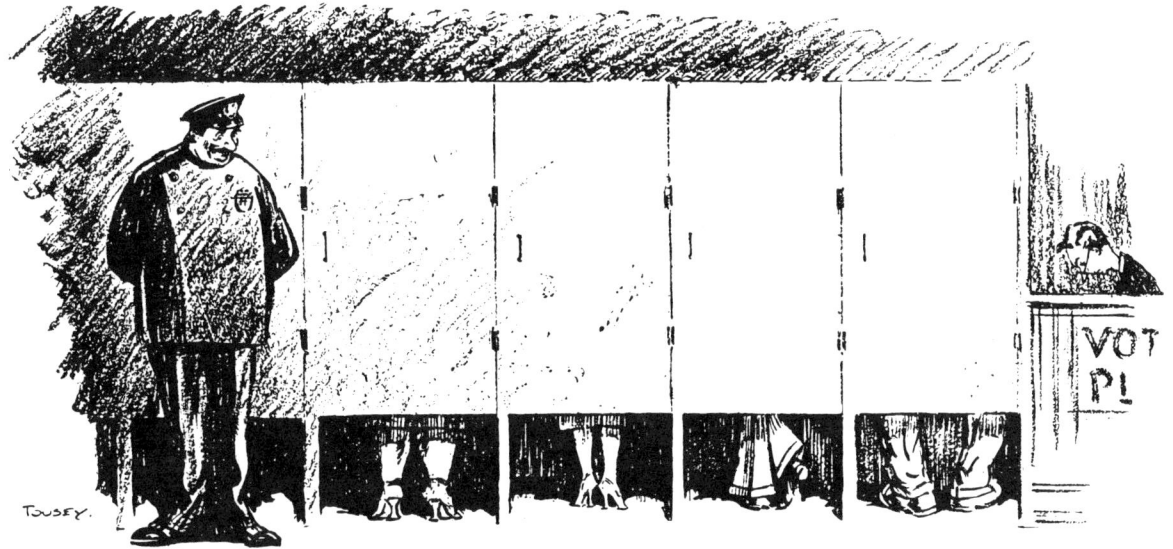

THE VOICE OF THE PEOPLE IS THE VOICE OF GOD

THE FIRST TOOTH

THE PHRASE TESTERS

DETERMINING THE POINT AT WHICH A MAN BECOMES "AS DRUNK AS A LORD."

A Reorder

"Ma says the last calf liver you sent was very nice, and would you send her another one from the same calf."

JACQUELINE: *They say I have a pagan body but a puritan mind.*
JACK: *Are you ever absent-minded?*

In the Hill Country

"Yes, indeed, Jim was always awful good to me. He shot me once, but that was only in fun."

KU KLUCKS

LADY GODIVA HAS HER HAIR BOBBED FOR THE OCCASION

LADY (to distinguished archaeologist): *And these cities—and things—and things— which you so laboriously—ah—exhume—can they be used again?*

HE: *Aren't you and the mistletoe on speaking terms?*
"Not in this jam. It's too much like kissing your brother good-by at a railroad station."

Christmas in Many Lands

SUSAN: *What is it, Mother? A sample?*

GENIAL SOUSE: *I don't care how late it is—I'm gonna solve this puzzle before I go home.*

YOUNG BRIDE (closing the Book of Etiquette): *Oh, dear, I don't know what to do! Here I have the minister coming to dinner and I simply* can't *find out if you should serve cocktails before or after grace.*

AT LAST—A PROPERLY PROPORTIONED DRESSING TABLE

THE CROSS WORD THAT SEPARATED PA FROM MA JONG

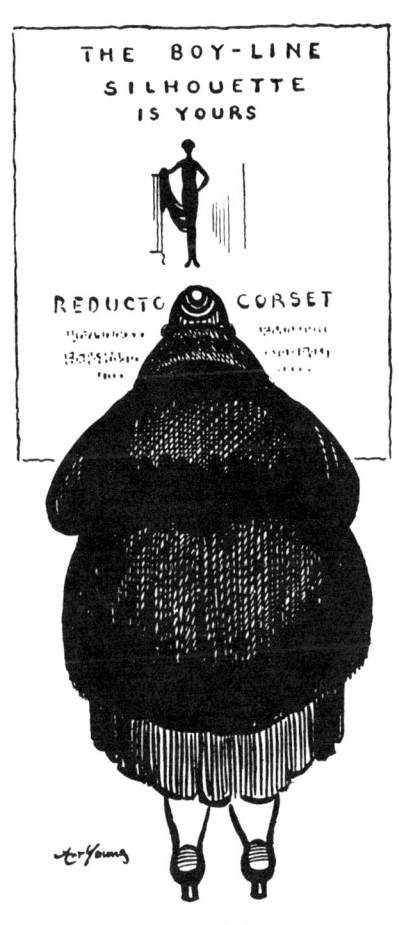

HOPE

THE PHRASE TESTERS

DETERMINING THE CELERITY OF SAYING "JACK ROBINSON."

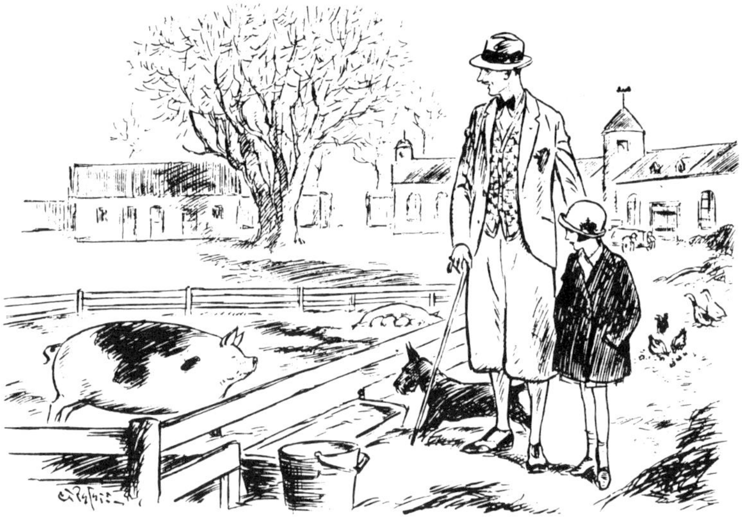

FATHER: *Do you know what that animal is?*
DAUGHTER: *Of course I do, it's a bank.*

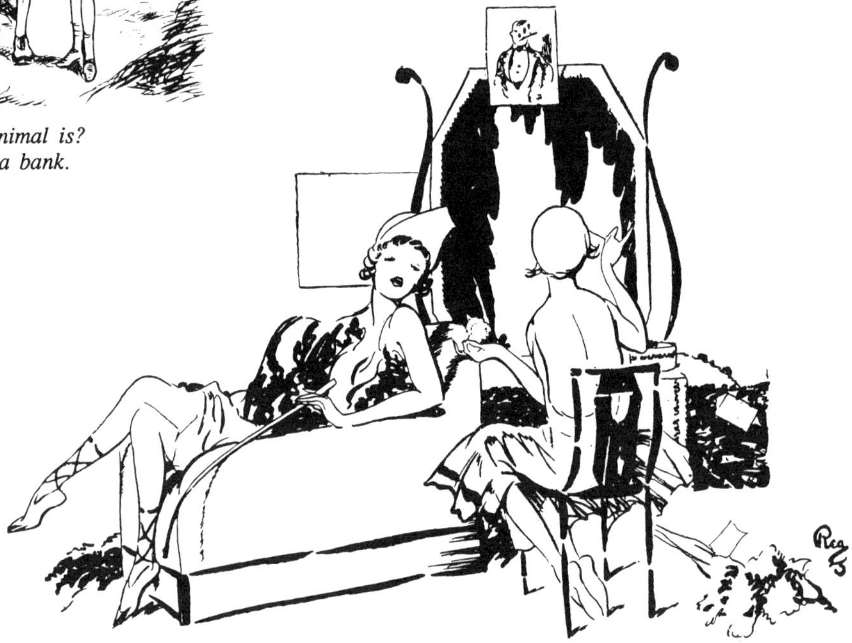

"Gee, Madge, y' don't mean t' tell me you're marrying th' guy?"
"Yeah. I found out he didn't have enough to pay me f'r bringin' breach o' promise, so I decided to let him do the right thing by me."

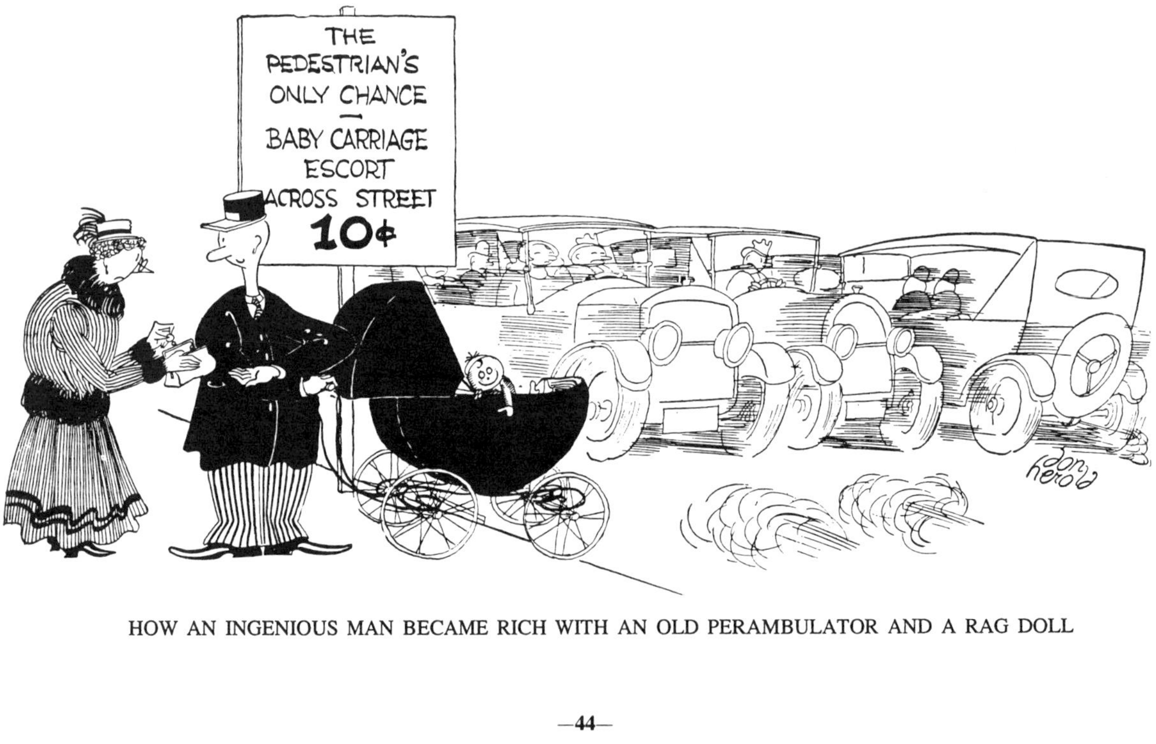
THE
PEDESTRIAN'S
ONLY CHANCE
BABY CARRIAGE
ESCORT
ACROSS STREET
10¢

HOW AN INGENIOUS MAN BECAME RICH WITH AN OLD PERAMBULATOR AND A RAG DOLL

IN YE GOODE OLDE DAYES

YE YNAUGURATYONE.

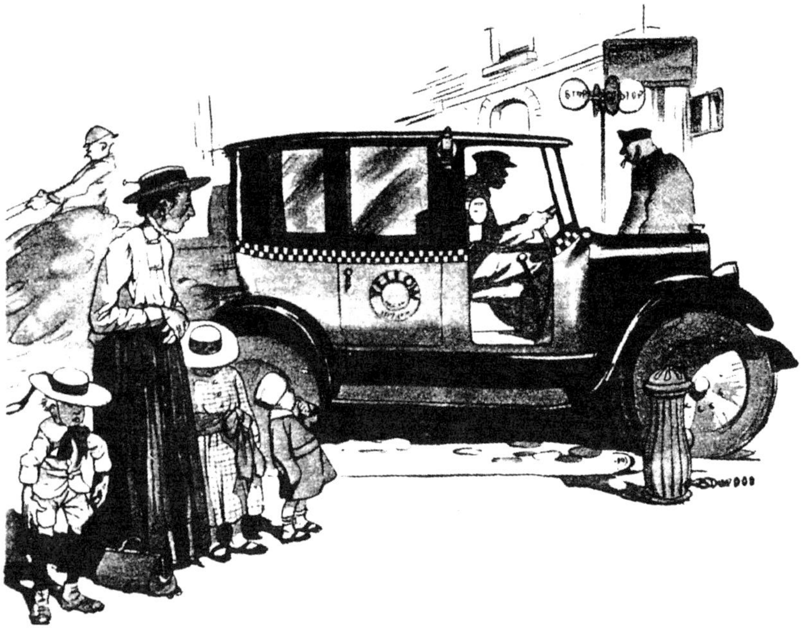

COUNTRY VISITOR: *Land sakes! Every time I come to town I see that car!*

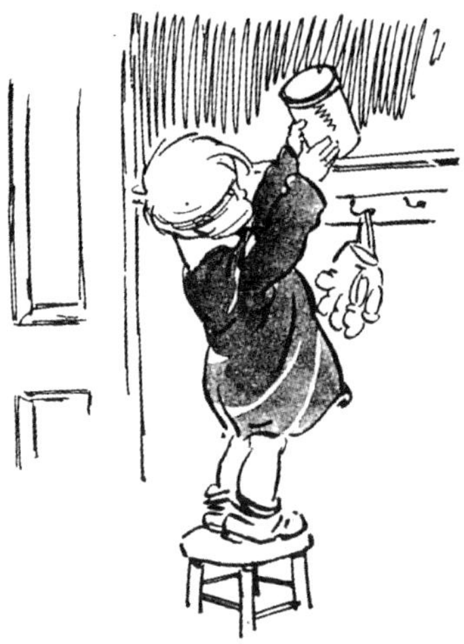

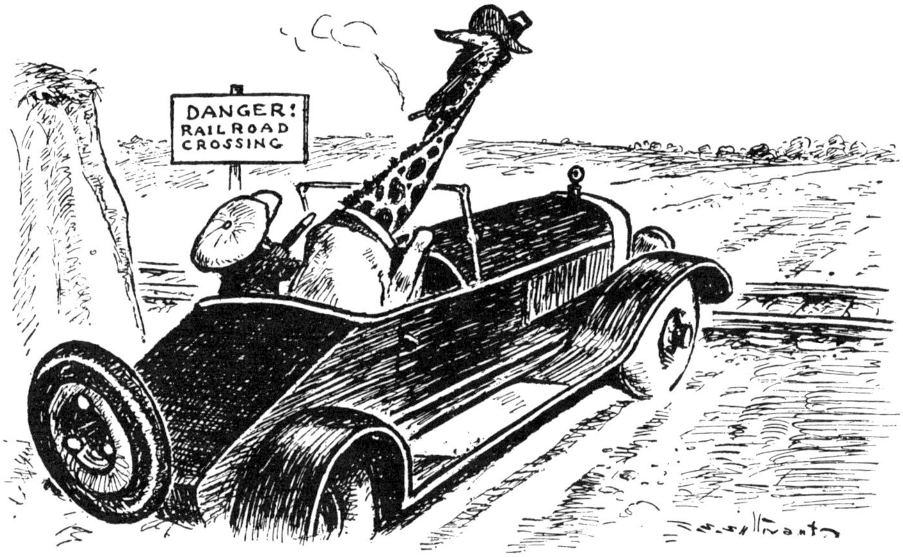
DANGER!
RAILROAD
CROSSING

GERALD GIRAFFE: *All right! Step on it.*

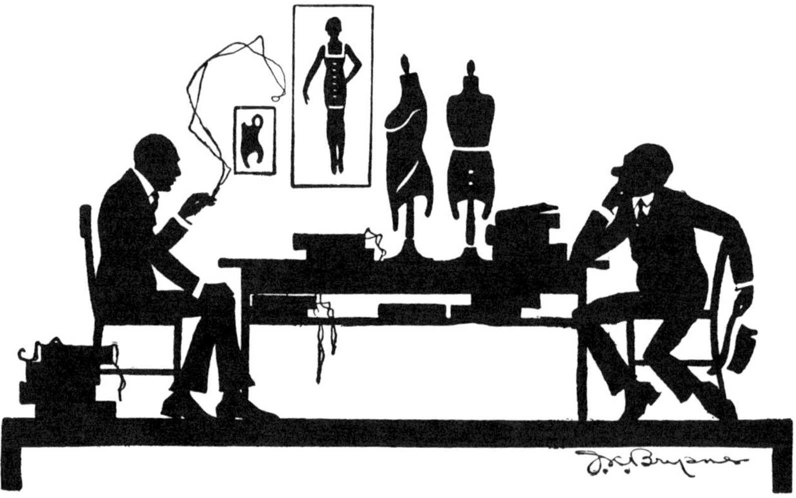

"How can I advertise my corsets?"
"Have you tried sending out a form letter?"

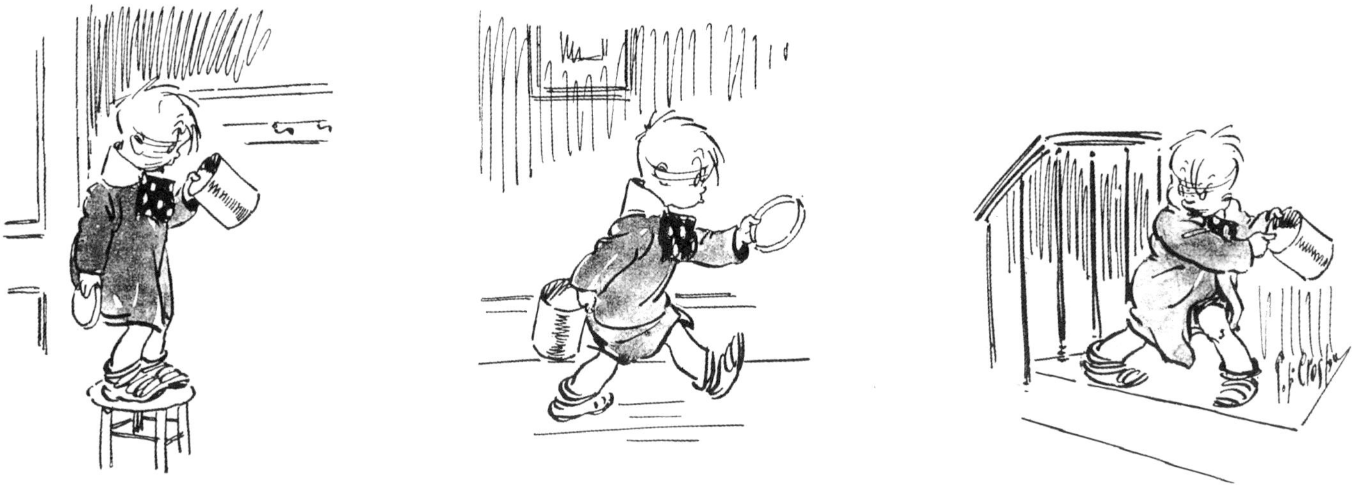

SKIPPY: *Who's been at my ants?*

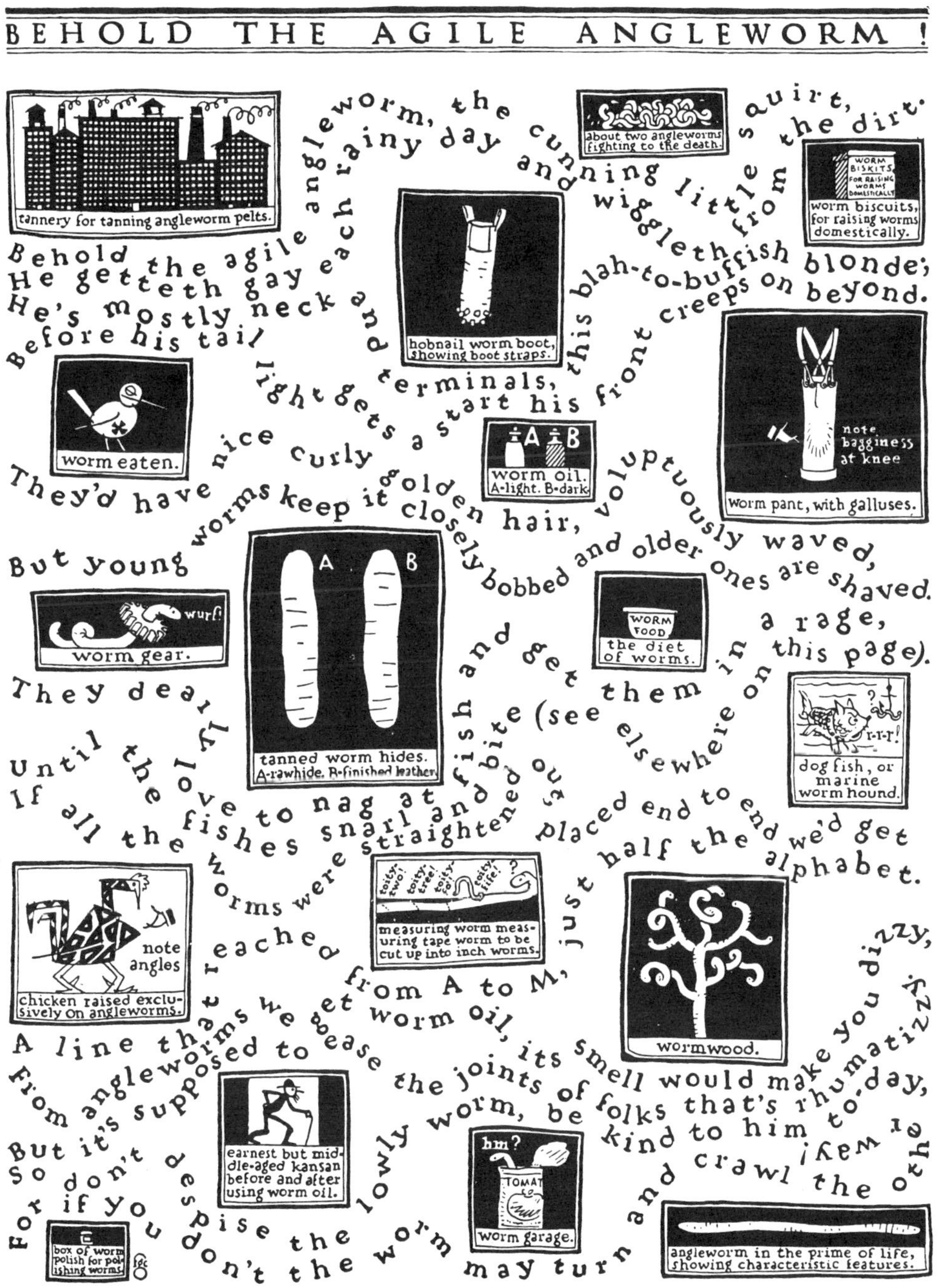

BEHOLD THE AGILE ANGLEWORM!
Behold the agile angleworm, the cunning little squirt,
He getteth gay each rainy day and wiggleth from the dirt.
He's mostly neck and terminals, this blah-to-buffish blonde;
Before his tail light gets a start his front creeps on beyond.
They'd have nice curly golden hair, voluptuously waved,
But young worms keep it closely bobbed and older ones are shaved.
They dearly love to nag at fish and get them in a rage,
Until the fishes snarl and bite (see elsewhere on this page).
If all the worms were straightened out, placed end to end we'd get
A line that reached from A to M, just half the alphabet.
From angleworms we get worm oil, its smell would make you dizzy,
But it's supposed to grease the joints of folks that's rhumatizzy,
So don't despise the lowly worm, be kind to him to-day,
For if you don't the worm may turn and crawl the other way.
tannery for tanning angleworm pelts.
about two angleworms fighting to the death.
WORM BISKITS FOR RAISING WORMS DOMESTICALLY
worm biscuits, for raising worms domestically.
hobnail worm boot, showing boot straps.
worm eaten.
A B
worm oil. A-light. B-dark
note bagginess at knee
worm pant, with galluses.
A B
tanned worm hides. A-rawhide. B-finished leather
wurf!
worm gear.
WORM FOOD
the diet of worms.
r-r-r!
dog fish, or marine worm hound.
note angles
chicken raised exclusively on angleworms.
toity-two! toity-tree! toity-for! toity-five?
measuring worm measuring tape worm to be cut up into inch worms.
wormwood.
earnest but middle-aged kansan before and after using worm oil.
hm?
TOMAT
worm garage.
box of worm polish for polishing worms.
angleworm in the prime of life, showing characteristic features.

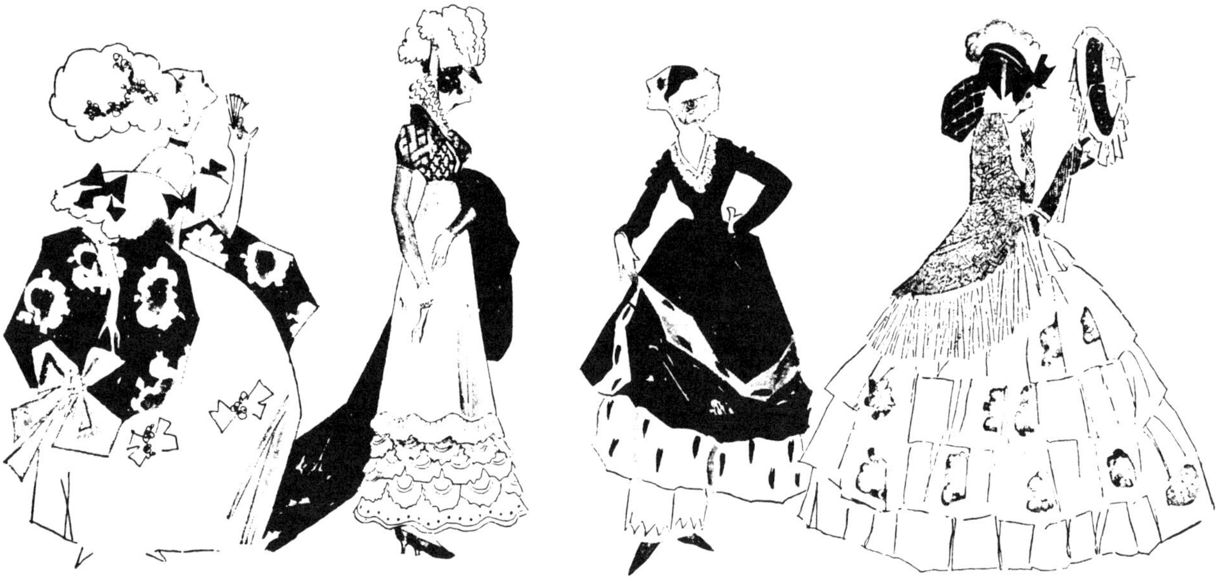

Daughters of the

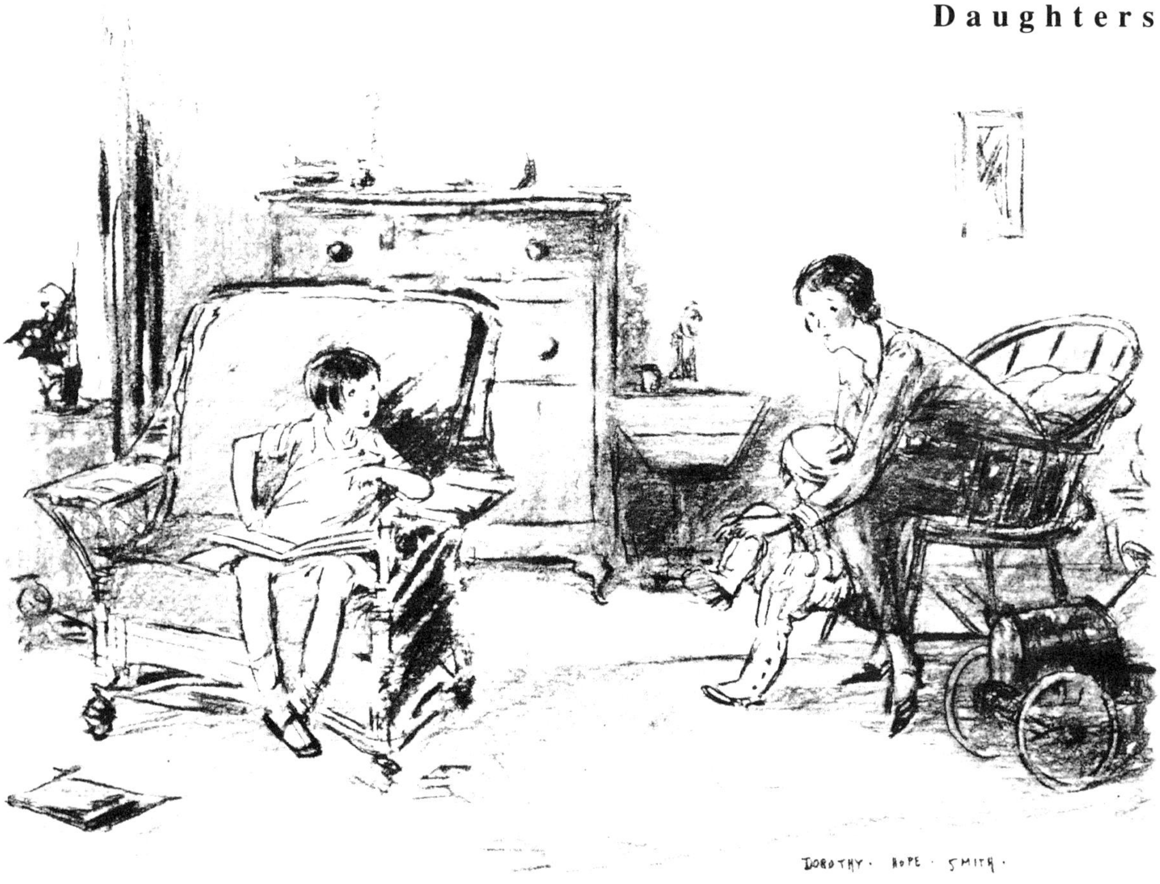
DOROTHY · HOPE · SMITH ·

DOROTHY: *I've looked all through this Mother Goose book, but I can't find that poem about "Little Bo-Peep Has Lost Her Sheik."*

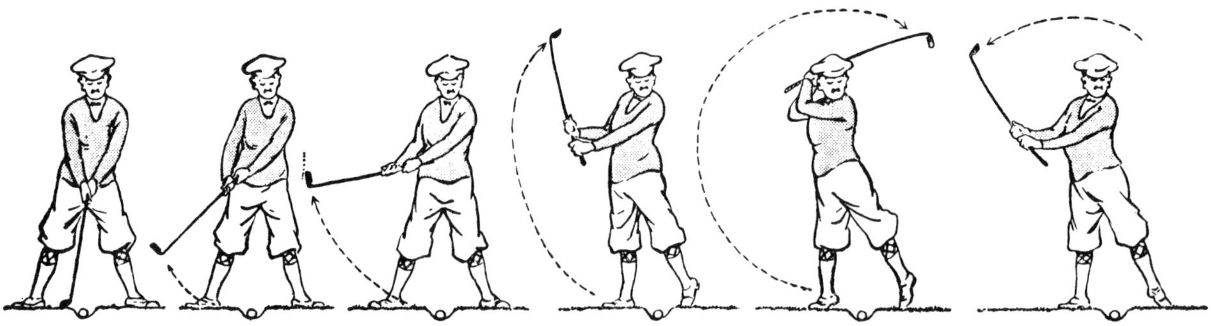

DIAGRAM SHOWING CORRECT METHOD

American Evolution

"What ho, smith! Bring me two quarts of heavy oil and I would fain have my grease cups turned down."

OF PLAYING FROM A BAD LIE

SKIPPY: *C'mon, show us somethin', I can't wait all day.*

DEACON SPRIGGS: *Young man, why do you spend so much of your time standing around on the station platform?*
YOUTH: *Wal, a feller gets tired of jes' doin' nothin'.*

RED GULCH TUNES IN ON THE BED-TIME STORY

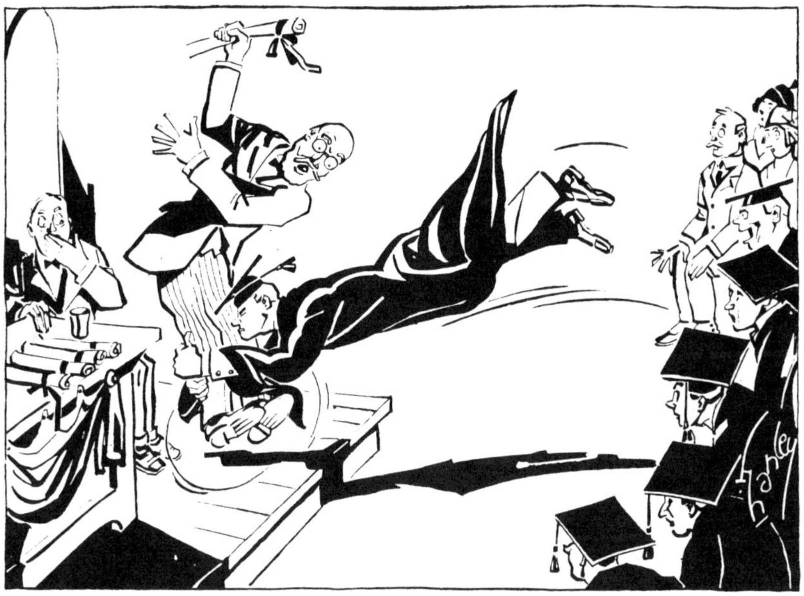

THE FELLOW WHO GOT THROUGH COLLEGE ON HIS FOOTBALL SUPREMACY TAKES HIS DIPLOMA

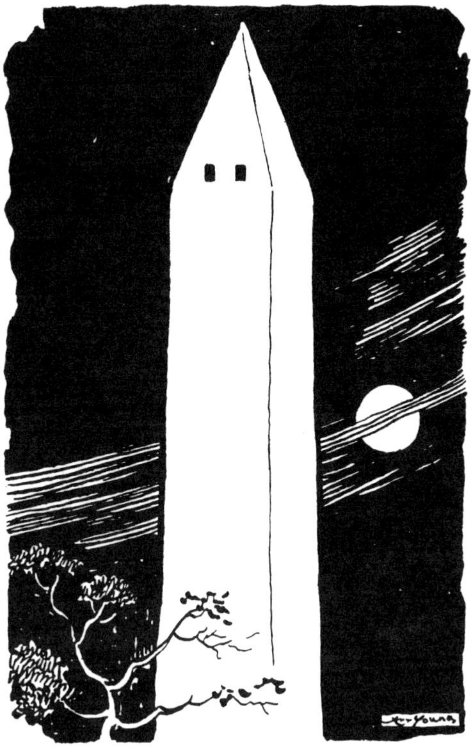

"The Ku Klux Klan have moved their headquarters to Washington."—NEWS ITEM.

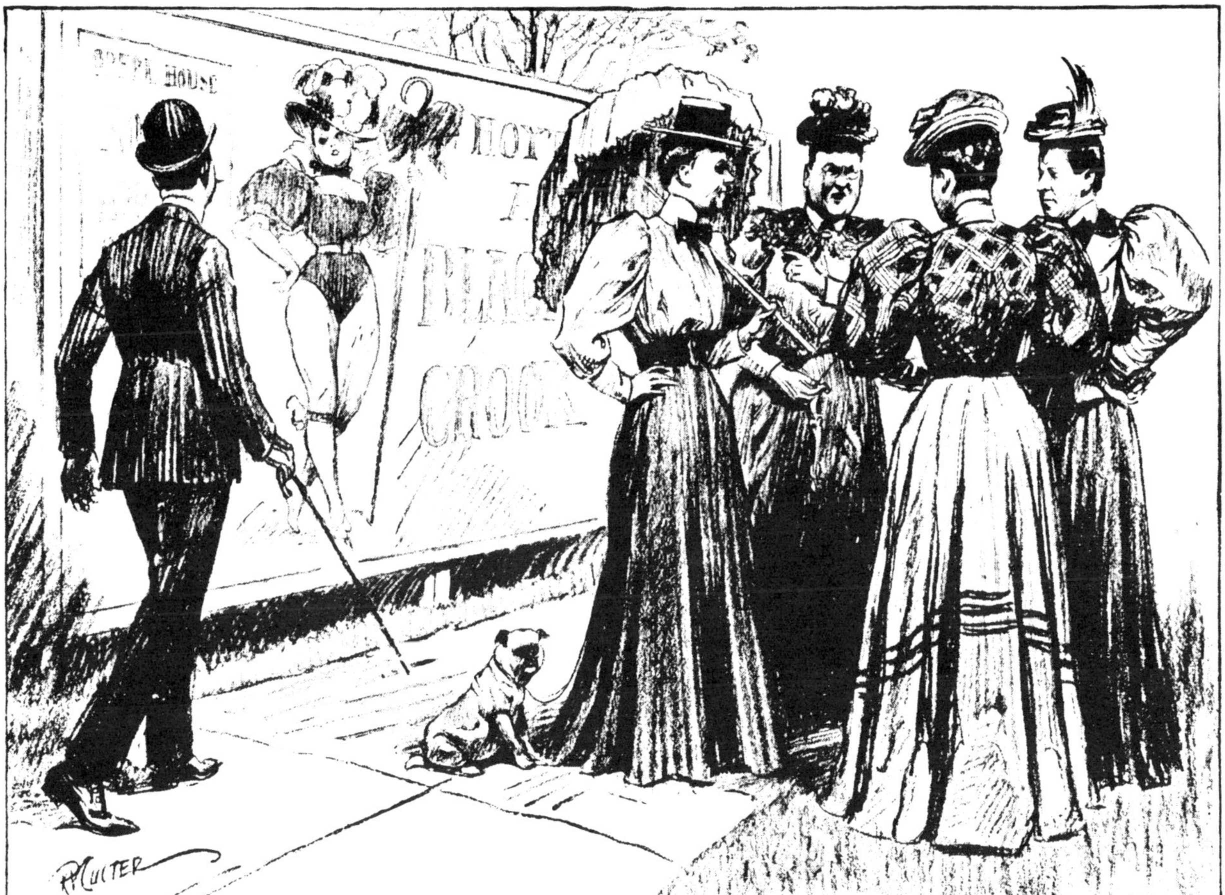

THE GAY NINETIES

OUTRAGED WOMANHOOD HOLDING AN IMPROMPTU INDIGNATION MEETING IN FRONT OF A BILLBOARD ADVERTISING THE FIRST ATTEMPT TO GLORIFY THE AMERICAN GIRL ON THE STAGE. ALSO SHOWING A HAPLESS MALE OF THE PERIOD ABOUT TO GO TO THE DEMNITION BOW-WOWS UNLESS SOMETHING IS DONE QUICKLY TO SAFEGUARD HIS MORALS.

AT THE MOMENT OF OPENING THE EVENING'S PROGRAM THE STAR ANNOUNCER SUFFERS AN ATTACK OF HICCOUGHS

ASSISTANT: *Well, what's th' row? Didn't you tell me you wanted me to get familiar with the typewriter?*

HARRIET: *I've bought a new gown and I'm frightfully in debt.*
AGATHA: *Head over ears?*
HARRIET: *No, it buttons down the front.*

HARK! HARK! THE HOG!

close-up of "our hero" in one of his proudest moments.

The pig's a fus-
Sy quadruped,
He wants a nice
Clean feather bed

"our hero" luxuriating in his fastidious bed.

With lace and rib-
Bons round about
And Eau de Co-
Logne on his snout.

"our hero" fastidiating in his luxurious toilette.

He wants his bris-
Tles combed just so,
His knuckles pol-
Ished till they glow.

"our hero" worrying himself thin over his personal appearance.

He really needs
A special steward
To keep his hoof-
Les manicured.

A pig should al-
Ways be garaged
Where he can have
His hips massaged;

a blind pig

Where he can get
His daily shave
And likewise too
His Marcel wave.

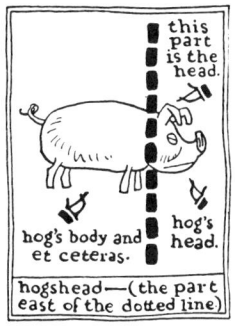
hogshead—(the part east of the dotted line)

A tepid bath
At half past nine.
At ten apply
"Shampoo de Swine".

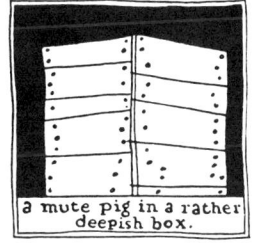
a mute pig in a rather deepish box.

By twelve fifteen
He's in the mood
To undertake
A bit of food.

"our hero" worrying over his table manners.

"our hero" demonstrating correct use of pig pen.

His lunch he can-
Not eat with zest
Without the mar-
Ket's very best.

pig "led"— (ha! ha! ha! ha! ha! ha! ha! ho! ho! ho! ho! ha! ho!)

Clear consommé,
Perhaps a slice
Of rich roast squab,
And then an ice.

pig's tie. (from "what the well-dressed ham will wear.")

His beauty sleep
Till three and then
An hour's saun-
Ter round the pen.

showing method of ironing pig with pig iron.

Perhaps a song.
Then at the door
To have his tea
And cakes, at four.

Now to the cor-
Ner by the logs
To chat with all
The other hogs

pickled pig's feet.

About the la-
Test fads in use.
For instance, "How
Does one reduce?"

pig's kin.

Thus pass his days,
The happy rogue!
Such are his whims,
His sense of vogue.

pigmy

Perhaps you had-
N't realized.
My dear! you'd real-
Ly be surprised.

embroidered silk purse made out of a sow's ear, showing that it can be done.

DT CARLISLE

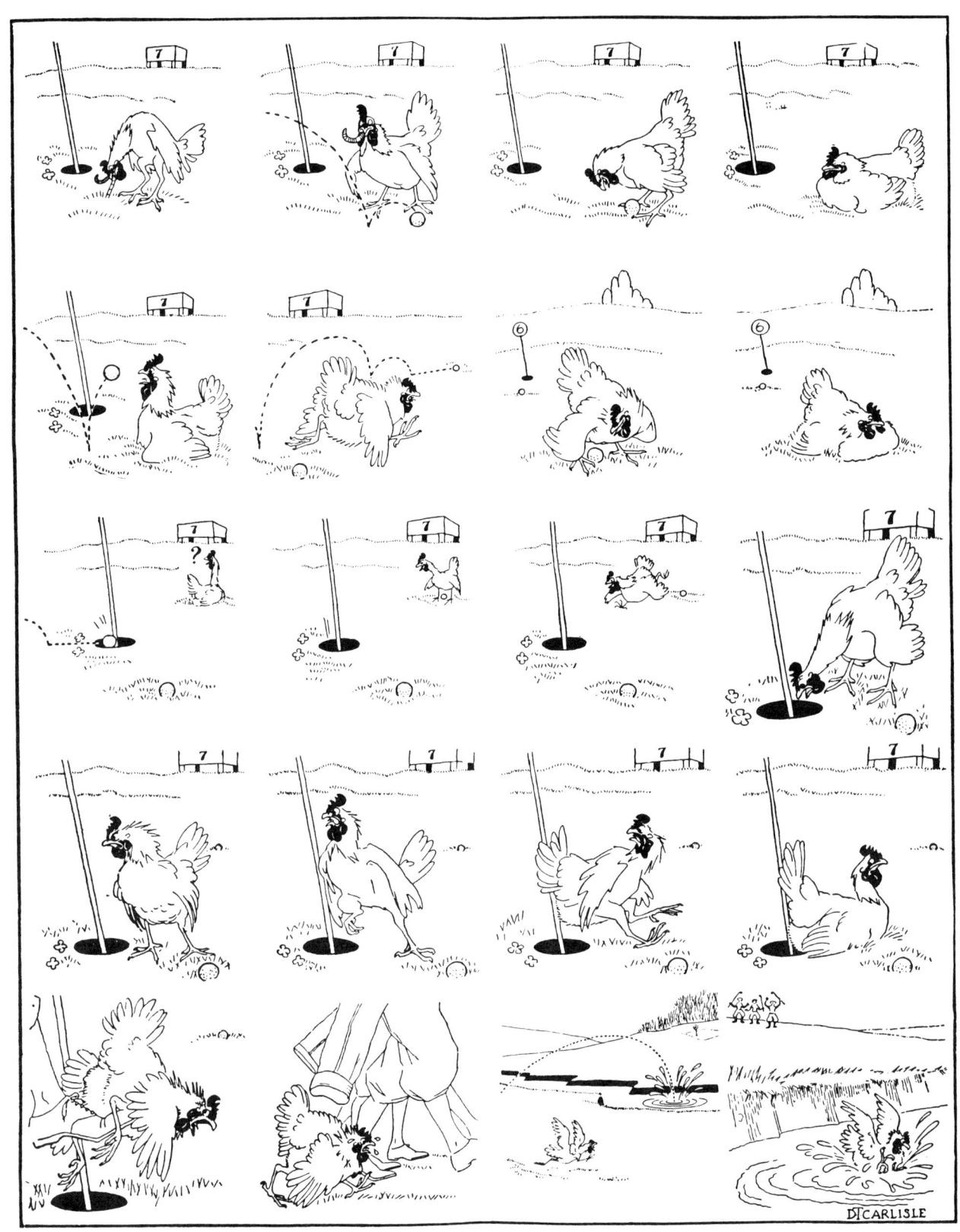

The Maternal Instinct.

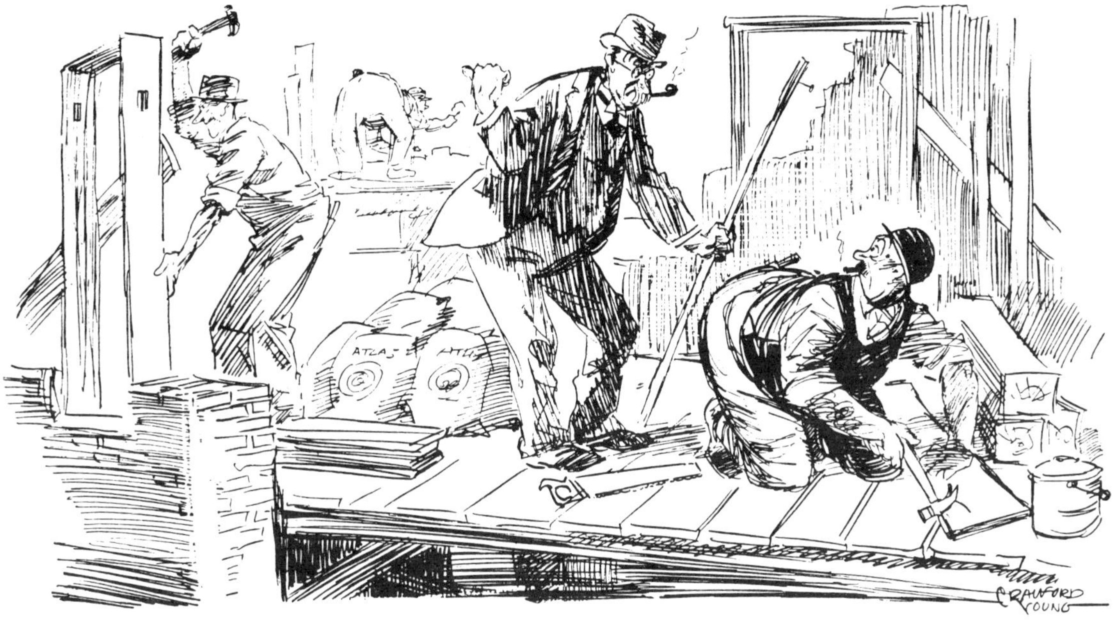
ATLAS
CRAWFORD YOUNG

FOREMAN: *Say, Thompson, that man is doing twice as much as you are.*
"Sure! I keep tellin' the poor sap but you can't learn him nothin'."

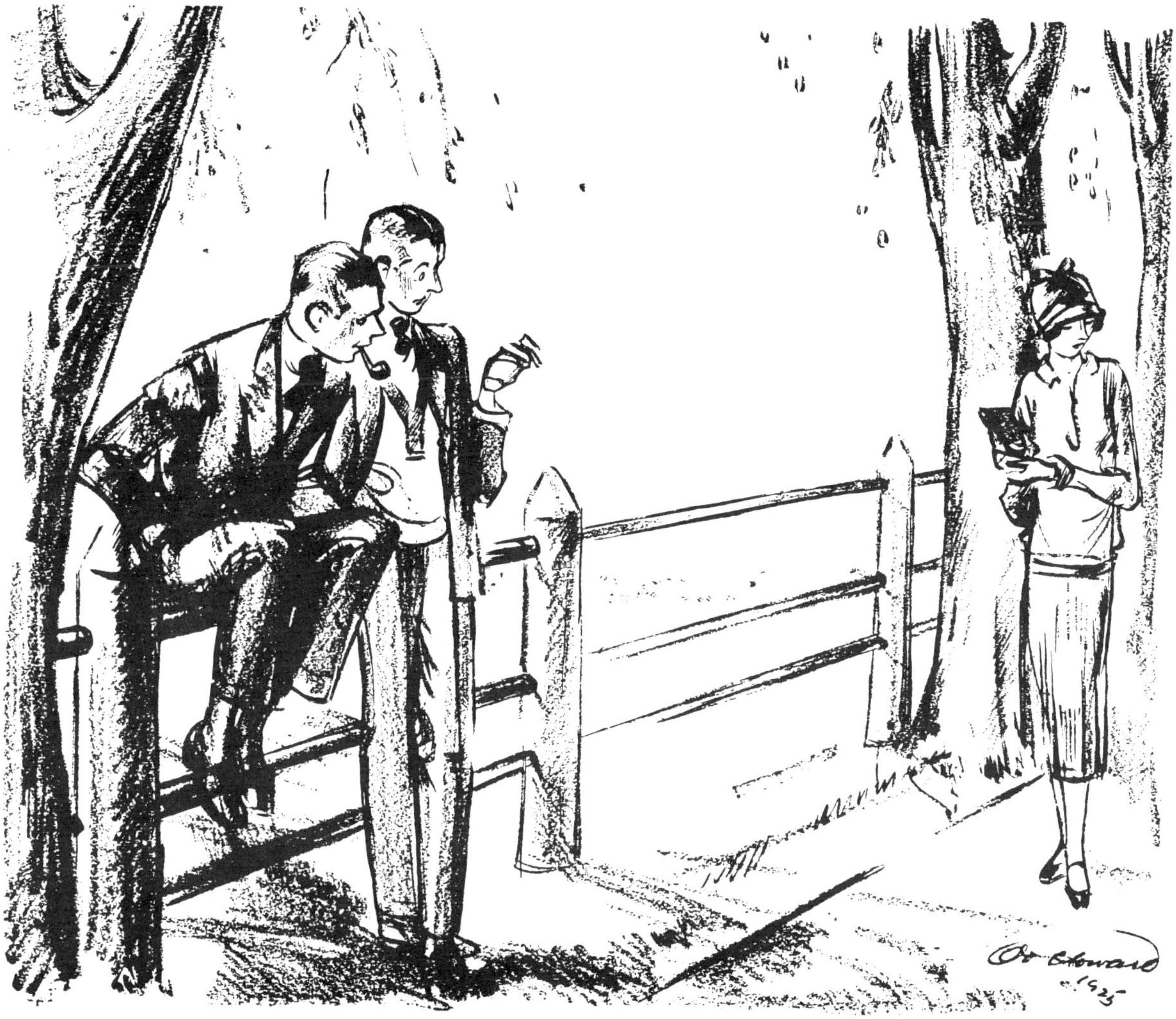

DESIRE UNDER THE ELMS

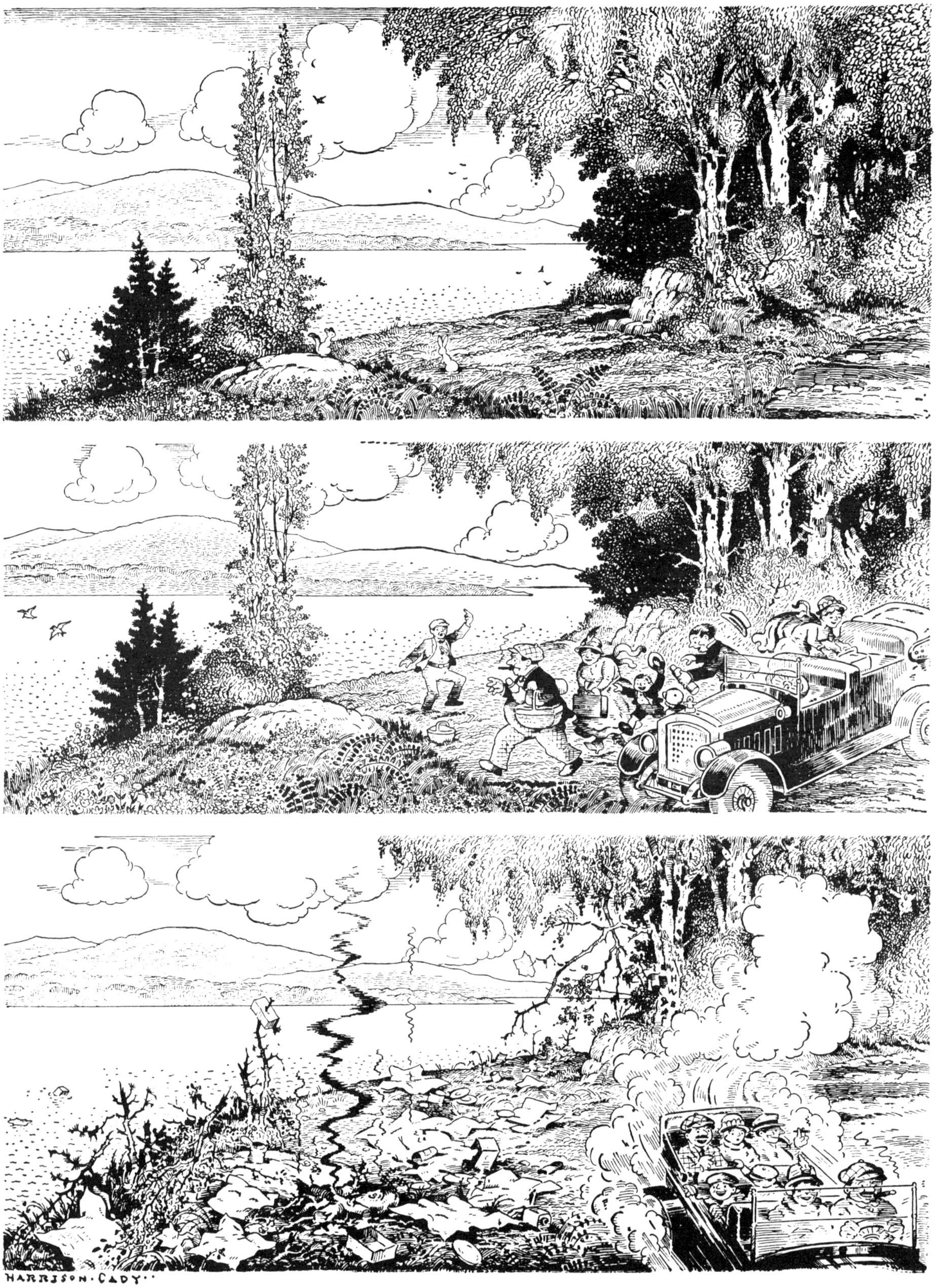
HARRISON·CADY

The Nature Lovers

ARTIST: *I say, buzz off—I'm not a bit in the mood for burglars.*

"What is the peculiar swishing sound I hear, Grandpop?"
"You're too young to recognize it—but I remember! That young lady is actually wearing a silk petticoat!"

"I feel like a glass o' beer, Bill."
"I wish you was, mate!"

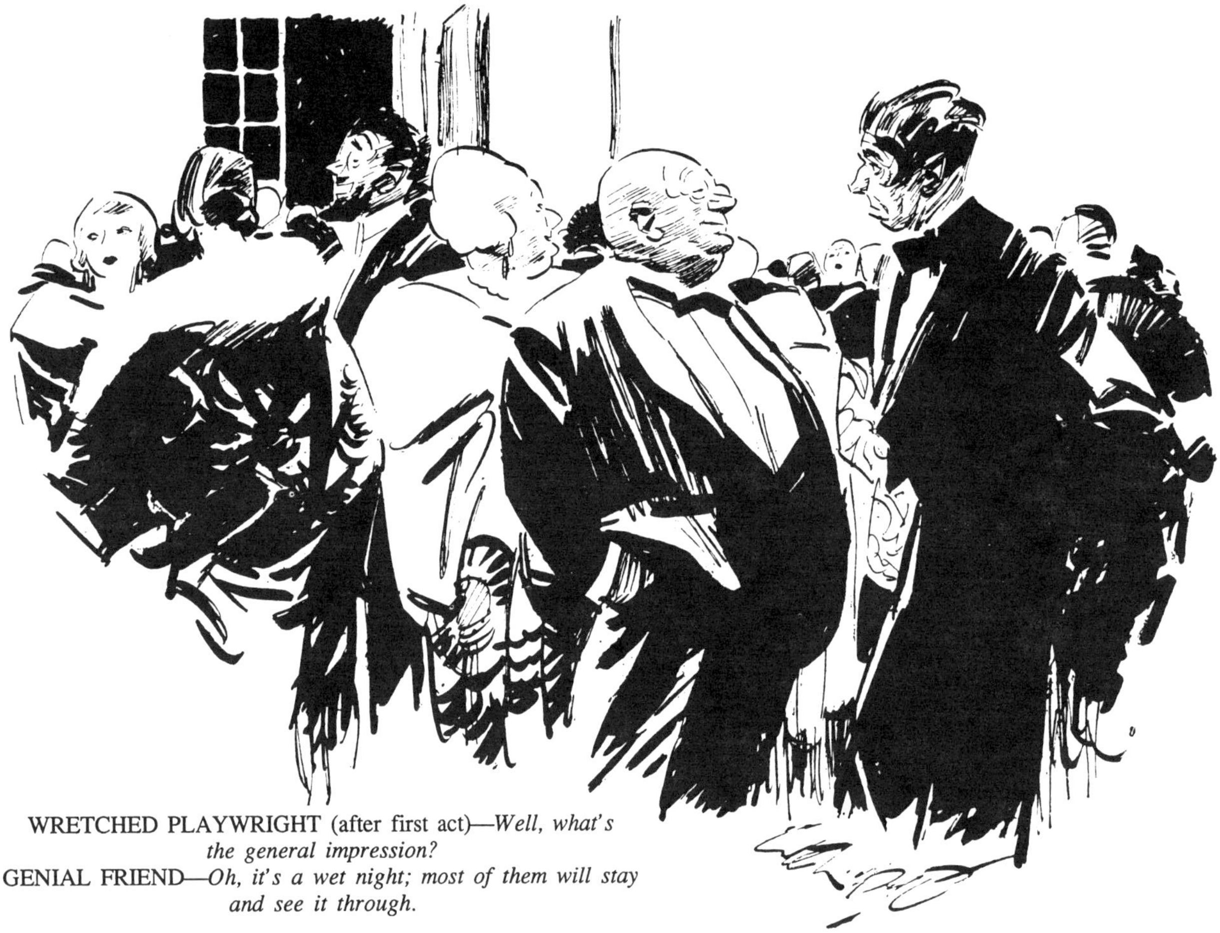

WRETCHED PLAYWRIGHT (after first act)—*Well, what's the general impression?*
GENIAL FRIEND—*Oh, it's a wet night; most of them will stay and see it through.*

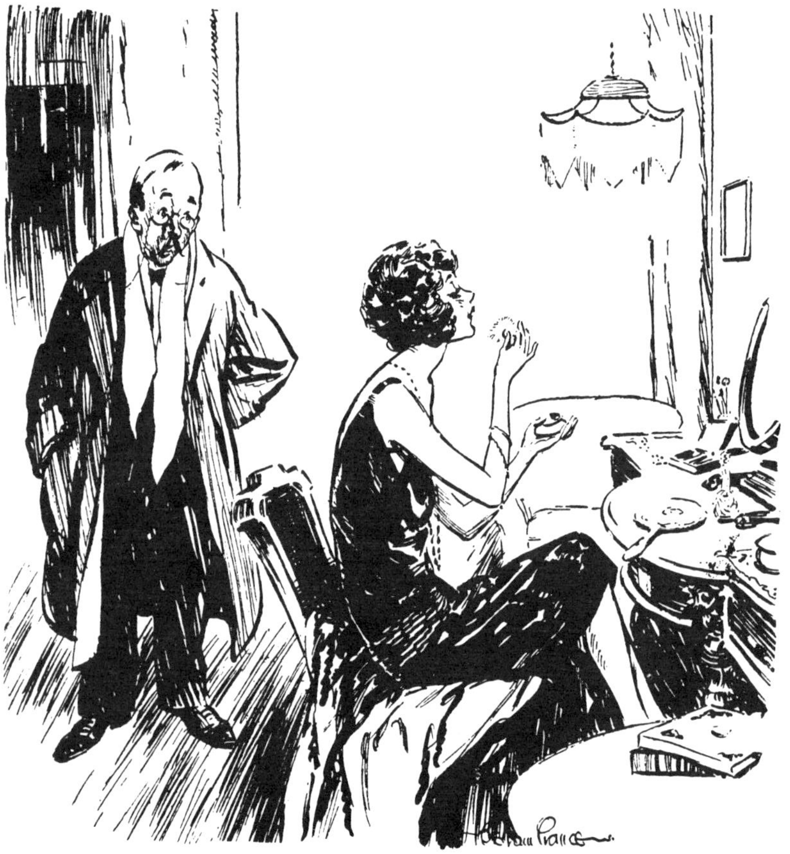

FATHER—*Your mother never dressed the way you girls do to-day to catch a husband.*
DAUGHTER—*No, but look what she got!*

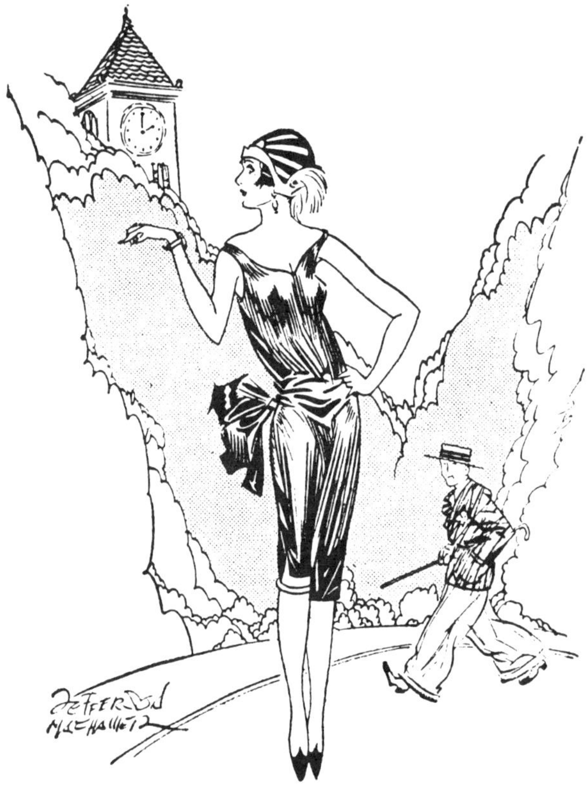

"My goo'ness—I'm fast!"

"I'm in love and I am loved."
"Then you must be perfectly happy."
"But it isn't the same man!"

THE LASS THAT LOVED A BOOTLEGGER.

"A little paint certainly makes a lot o' difference, don't it, mum?"

RED HOT MAMMA!

In Code
"What's he talking about?"
"I don't know. He doesn't say."

TRIX: *I can't find my bathing suit anywhere.*
"Have you looked in your handbag, dear?"

ALL SUMMER MAGAZINE COVERS MAY BE BATHING GIRLS, BUT NOT ALL BATHING GIRLS ARE SUMMER MAGAZINE COVERS.

"A painter asked her to pose for the figure, and she insisted upon wearing a necklace."
"The prude!"

SCOTLAND DECIDES TO SET AN EXAMPLE OF MODESTY

THE HEIGHT OF INDIFFERENCE—LADY GODIVA VISITS ATLANTIC CITY

HE: *I go mad when I think of you dancing with other men. Supposing I danced with other women?*
SHE: *I know the position is terrible—they'd go mad, probably.*

CHARLIE CHAPLIN TEACHES HIS NEW SON HOW TO "WALK."

PEGGY: *I've lost my purse.*
POLLY: *Never mind, it doesn't show.*

DIRECTOR: *Say, girls, don't put on those one-piece suits; you're going to wear crinolines instead—Will Hays is visiting the studio to-day.*

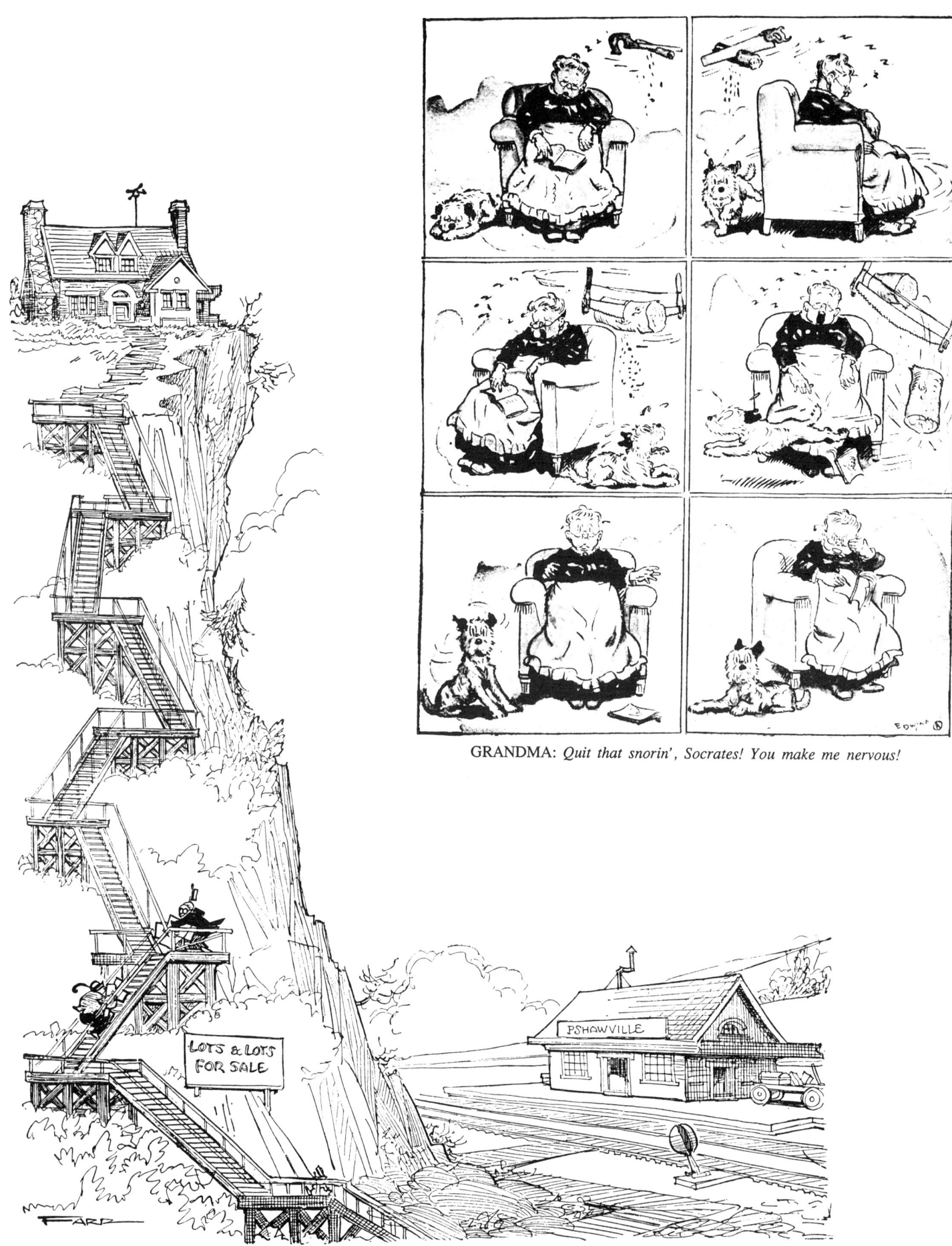

GRANDMA: *Quit that snorin', Socrates! You make me nervous!*

THE REAL-ESTATE AGENT SAID THAT THE BUNGALOW WAS "JUST A STONE'S THROW FROM THE STATION."

Time: 3 a.m.
"Mother told me not to come home with the milkman."
"Oh—doesn't she know I'm a bond salesman?"

"Bill! She's got two sets of garters on!"
"Sure, they're all wearing 'em now—one pair to hold up their stockings and the other to hold up traffic."

ARTIST: *Thought I'd do a little landscape painting around here.*
JOSHUA: *Don't think ye'll find much fer pictures, mister. They was a photograph-feller up here last year, and he tuk about everything.*

"Good morning!"
"Good night!"

URSULA: *Is my nose shiny, dearie?*
LAMBERT: *No, but your right knee is dusty.*

VISITING RACCOON: *I suppose you'll soon be sending your son to college.*
MAMMA RACCOON: *Me? Not Much! I didn't raise my boy to be an overcoat.*

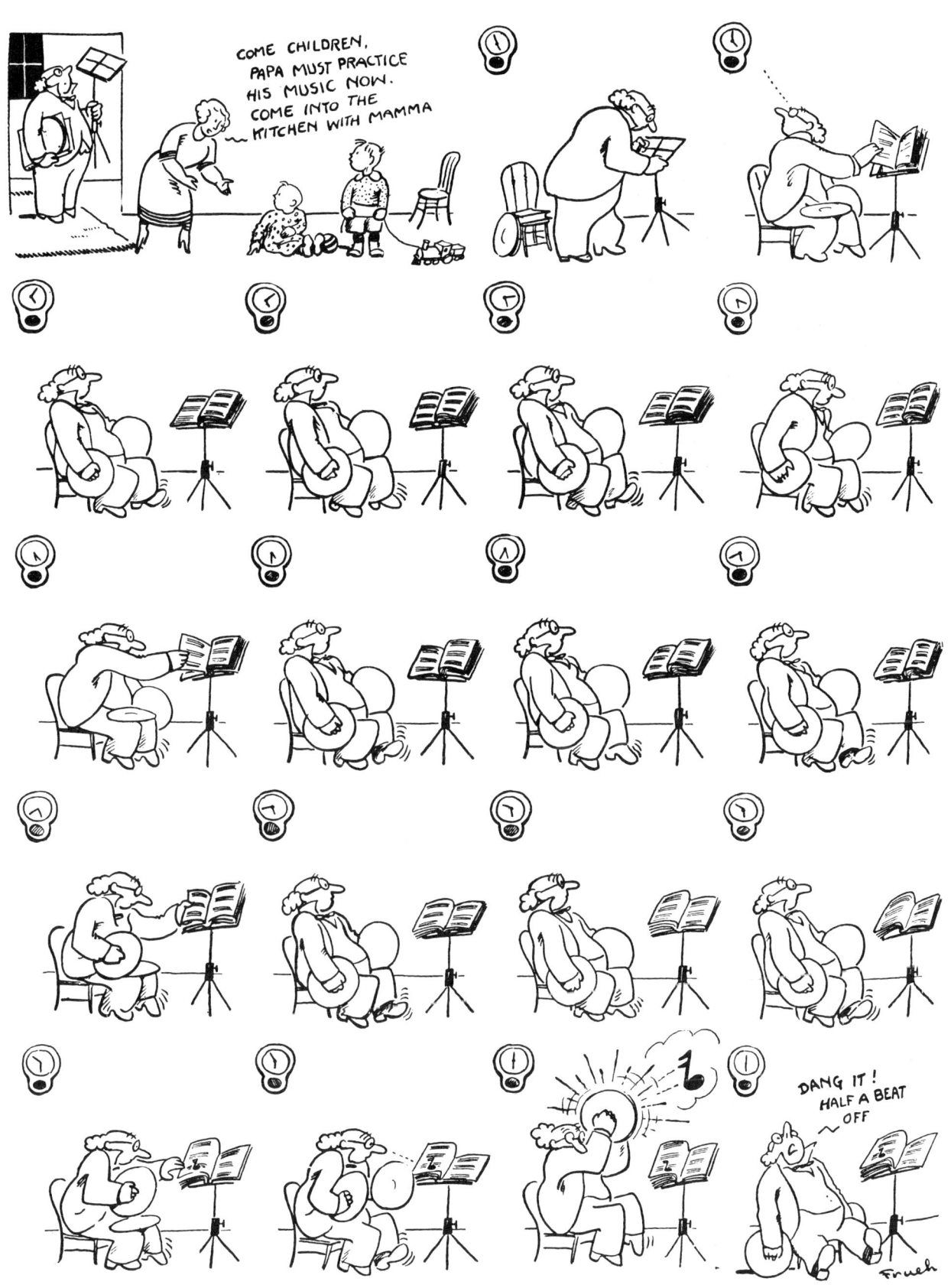

The Cymbal Player Practices at Home

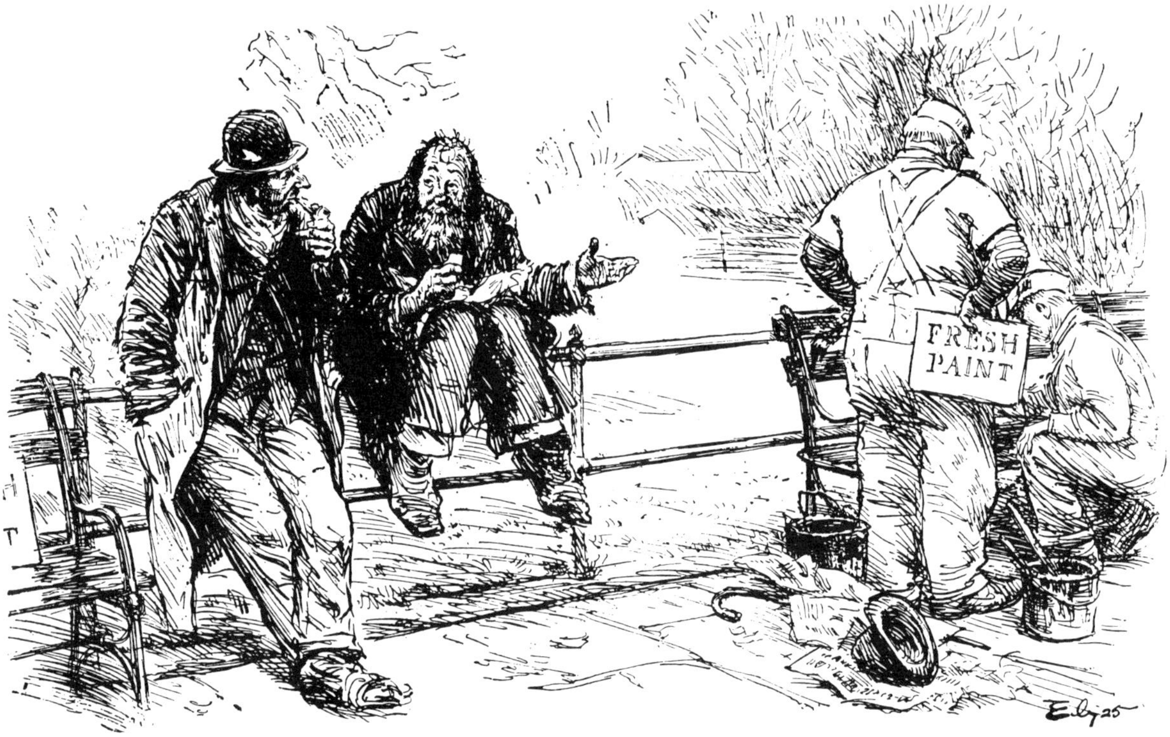
FRESH PAINT

"Of course, it's awfully messy now, but the place simply had to be done over!"

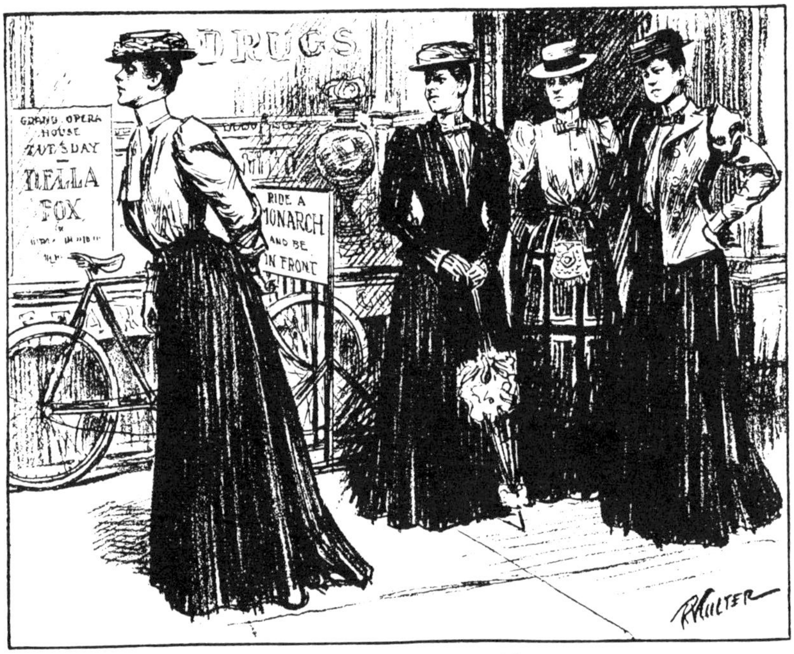
DRUGS
GRAND OPERA HOUSE

THE GAY NINETIES

THE LAST WORD IN COMPLIMENTS

"What's the matter with Etta Purdy? She hardly spoke to us."
"Oh, she's been that way ever since somebody called her a Gibson Girl."

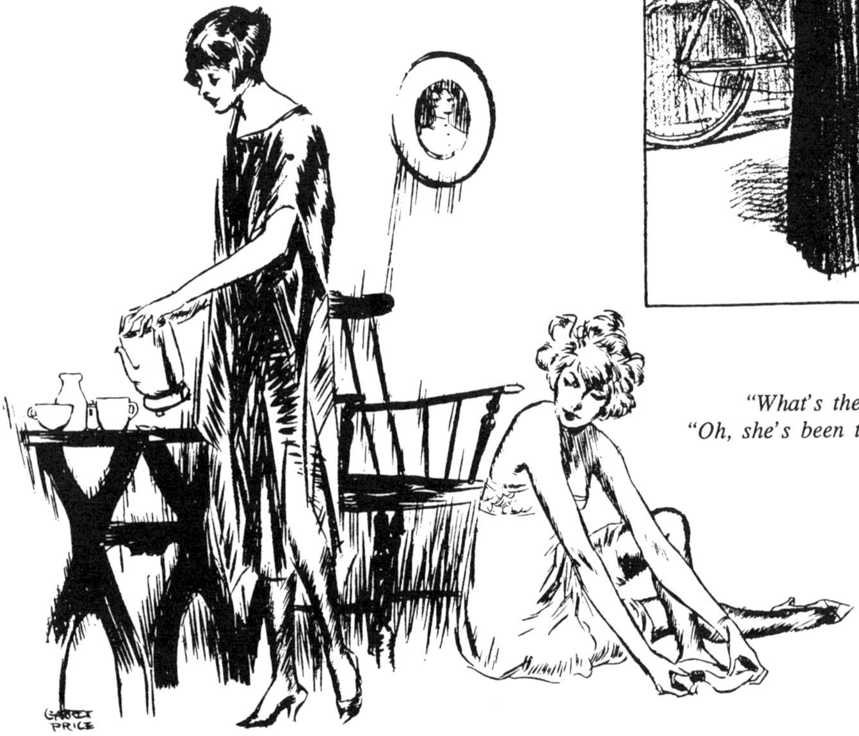

"How's your new department manager?"
"Not bad—if she was a man, I think I'd actually like her."

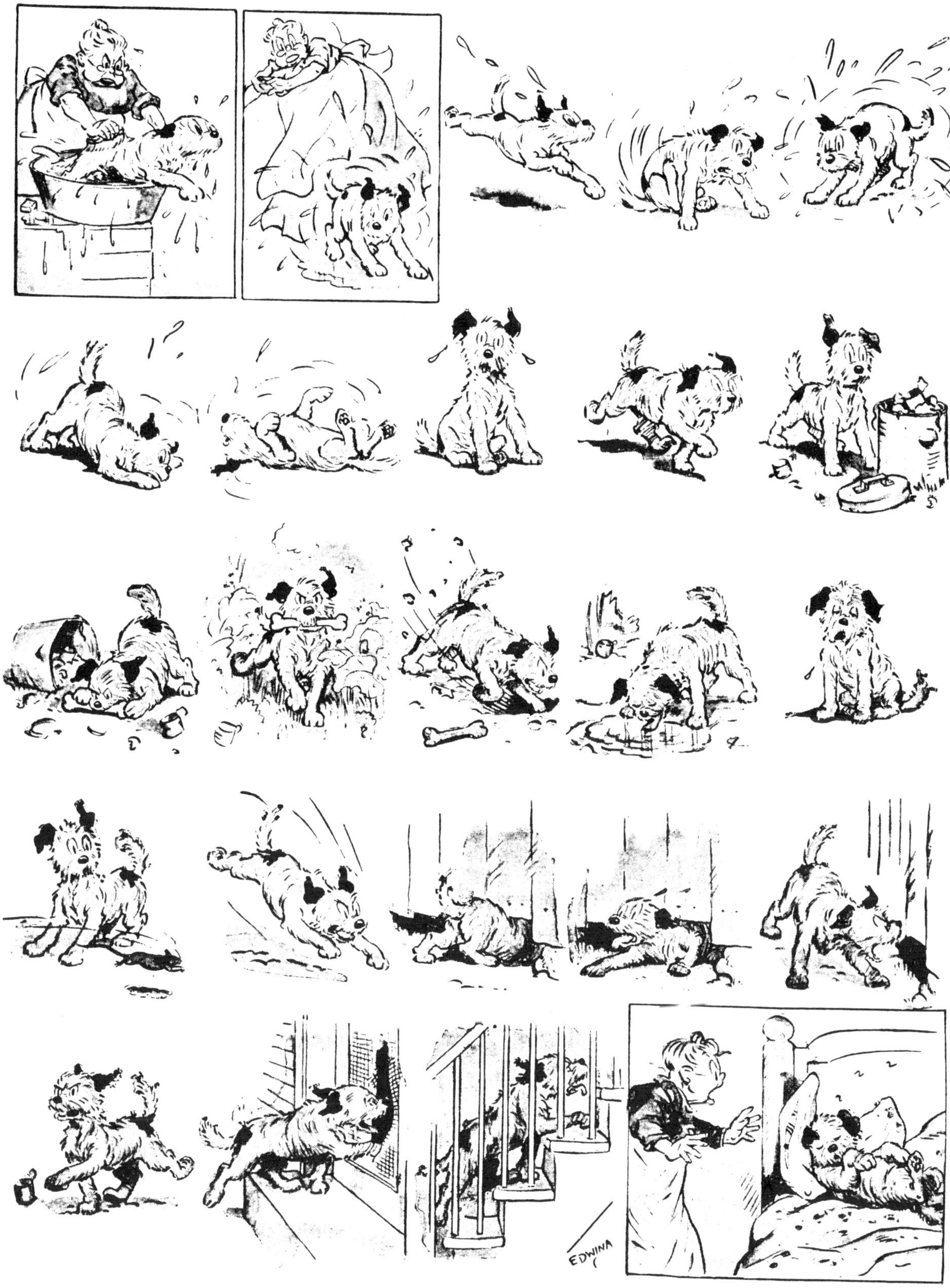
EDWINA

Wash Day

SUGGESTED LINE MARKINGS BETWEEN STREET CROSSINGS, SO PEDESTRIANS MAY KNOW HOW THEY ARE PROGRESSING TOWARD THEIR GOAL.

THE EFFICIENCY EXPERT'S CUFF

Have You a Little Peter Pan in Your Home?
MOTHER (TO NURSE): *At six o'clock tune in on the bedtime story from Pittsburgh, then play "Rock-a-Bye, Baby" and "Now I Lay Me" on the victofone.*

WOMAN'S WORK IS NEVER DONE

THE GAY NINETIES

CHRISTMAS MORNING AT JAKE'S PLACE DOWN ON THE CORNER, WHERE HOT TOM AND JERRYS WERE "ON THE HOUSE" TO OLD CUSTOMERS. THIS SESSION USUALLY LASTED UNTIL SOMEBODY'S LITTLE WILLIE ARRIVED WITH THE MESSAGE, "MAMMA SAYS PAPA IS TO COME RIGHT STRAIGHT HOME—THE TURKEY'S ON THE TABLE."

MAGAZINE EDITOR: *I thought I told you to put some snow in that background—don't you know what a Christmas cover is yet?*

"I don't see how I can fill them any better."

ANOTHER BOBBED-HAIR BANDIT

WITH BEST WISHES FOR A HAPPY NEW YEAR!